IN DEFIANCE OF HITLER

IN DEFIANCE OF
HITLER
THE SECRET MISSION OF
VARIAN FRY

CARLA KILLOUGH McCLAFFERTY

FARRAR STRAUS GIROUX ✳ NEW YORK

The author gratefully acknowledges Justus Rosenberg,
Professor Emeritus of Languages and Literature,
Bard College, for his expert reading of the manuscript.

Quotations from *Assignment: Rescue, An Autobiography* by Varian Fry,
copyright © 1945 by Varian Fry; copyright © 1968 by Annette R. Fry.
Reprinted by permission of Scholastic Inc.
Quotations from *Surrender on Demand* by Varian Fry, copyright © 1945 by Varian Fry;
copyright © 1997 by Sylvia Fry and James Fry.
Reprinted by permission of Johnson Books.
Quotations from the Varian Fry Papers, housed at the Rare Book and Manuscript
Library, Columbia University. Reprinted by permission of Annette Fry.

www.fsgkidsbooks.com

Library of Congress Cataloging-in-Publication Data
McClafferty, Carla Killough, 1958–
    In defiance of Hitler : the secret mission of Varian Fry / Carla Killough McClafferty.
    —1st ed.
        p.   cm.
    ISBN-13: 978-0-374-38204-9
    ISBN-10: 0-374-38204-2
    1. Fry, Varian, 1907–1967.   2. World War, 1939–1945—Jews—Rescue—France.
3. Holocaust, Jewish (1939–1945)—France.   4. Righteous Gentiles in the Holocaust—
United States—Biography.   5. War correspondents—United States—Biography.
I. Title.

D804.66.F79M33   2008
940.53'15092—dc22
[B]
                                                                    2007033271

Frontispiece: Varian Fry at his desk in the office of the American Relief Center.

This book is dedicated to the memory of the men and women who risked their lives to save others at the time when Adolf Hitler dominated most of Europe

CONTENTS

A NOTE TO THE READER

There are two accepted spellings for the city in France where Varian Fry worked: Marseille, the French spelling, and Marseilles, the usual spelling in English-speaking countries. The Spanish town of Portbou is also spelled Port Bou or Port-bou.

The city of Vichy was the location of the new French government created after Nazi Germany defeated France during World War II. The entire government, which collaborated with the Germans from that time on, became known as "Vichy."

In this book, Varian Fry visits both the American Embassy and the American Consulate. The embassy was located in Vichy and was the home of the ambassador of the United States to France. The ambassador represented the President of the United States. In other cities around France, including Marseilles, there were smaller offices called consulates that were under the supervision of the embassy. The job of the American Consulate was to help American citizens and issue visas.

Many refugees climbed the Pyrenees Mountains on foot to cross the border into Spain. The amount of time it took them varied, depending on such factors as the difficulty of the terrain at the location where they crossed, and the physical condition of each individual.

Numerous people worked with Varian Fry while he was in Marseilles, and it is unknown how he met most of them. Some helped Varian secretly rescue refugees; others worked in the office of the American Relief Center and knew nothing about his rescue work. In a book of this size, it is impossible to include everyone who participated in Varian Fry's work. That they are not mentioned by name in these pages in no way diminishes their contribution.

—C.K.M.

IN DEFIANCE OF HITLER

[Witness]

Varian Fry saw the mob. They gathered in front of the neat shops and cafés that lined Kurfürstendamm, one of Berlin's main streets. He heard singing in the distance. The melody was that of a German military song, but the words were chanted like a cheer at a ball game as more and more of the crowd joined in. A leader sang a line of the song, then the crowd repeated it.

Varian understood German well enough to realize the words meant:

When Jewish blood spurts from the knife,
Then everything will be fine again.

Somewhere in the crowd, someone yelled out "Jew." A pack of people surrounded the man who had been pointed out. They spit on the nameless "Jew," insulted him, and knocked him down onto the sidewalk. Once he was on the ground, the mob kicked him repeatedly, with sickening thuds. Then, from all directions, like a disease that spread, Varian heard "Jew," "Jew," "Jew." Each time a Jewish man or woman was pointed out, he or she was immediately set upon and beaten. The sound of sobbing women added to the chaos of shuffling feet and the repeating chorus of the military song. Then a new anti-Semitic chant rang out: "The best Jew is a dead Jew."

The mass of people on the street forced passing cars and buses to stop. If the occupants looked as if they might be Jewish, the crowd pulled them out and beat them. They pulled Jewish customers from cafés and attacked them. Everywhere Varian looked, Jewish people covered with blood ran down the street. Their pursuers were right behind them, hitting them with clubs and calling them names.

Members of the S.A., short for Sturmabteilung, the private Nazi army known as storm troopers, picked up tables and chairs from outside cafés and threw them through the windows of Jewish-owned shops.

Varian was horrified at what he was seeing.

"This is a holiday for us," a German youth said to Varian.

Varian was shocked when he realized that the people in the crowd were actually enjoying their brutal behavior. He looked at the people who made up the mob. They were German boys and girls, men and women, policemen and S.A. men, young and old, rich and poor. All sang and participated in the riot.

The scene Varian witnessed was seared into his memory.

The next morning, Varian walked down the once-charming street to survey the damage from the previous night. Shards of glass from broken shop windows littered the sidewalks and crunched beneath his feet. He passed several people who were bound with bandages.

Varian Fry had gone to Berlin to find out if the Germans were

A parade of S.A. troopers through the streets of Berlin in 1935. Within the S.A., a small group who acted as Hitler's bodyguards became known as the S.S. (an abbreviation of Schutzstaffel, meaning "protective echelon"). Ultimately the black-uniformed S.S. replaced the S.A.

Adolf Hitler designed the Nazi flag: a black swastika within a white disc on a blood-red background. The swastika had been an ancient symbol of prosperity, used by many different cultures around the world. In 1920 Hitler turned it into a Nazi symbol.

The people in the crowd have their hands raised in a Nazi salute. In everyday life, German citizens greeted each other this way, saying "Heil Hitler" (hail, or praise, Hitler). Sometimes, in a crowd, Germans chanted "Sieg Heil" (hail, or praise, to victory).

mistreating their own Jewish citizens. Ever since Adolf Hitler took over the government, rumors of abuse had spread throughout the world. As editor at *The Living Age*, a political journal, Varian wanted to see the situation for himself. Now he had no doubt. Germany had begun a reign of violence against Jews.

Hitler rose to power within the Nazi political party and was named Chancellor—the head of government—of Germany in 1933. The next year he added the title of *der Führer*, which means "the leader." As the supreme leader of Germany, Hitler became a dictator with unlimited power. Nothing happened in that country without his consent and approval.

Varian made an appointment with Ernst Hanfstaengl, who was chief of the Foreign Press Division of the Nazi Propaganda Ministry and a personal friend of Hitler's. Hanfstaengl—son of a German father and American mother—often entertained Hitler by playing classical music on the piano. Varian had never met Hanfstaengl, but they had one thing in common: they were both Harvard graduates.

Though their meeting took place in Berlin, Germany's capital, Hanfstaengl spoke to Varian in English. In his cultured accent, he calmly explained that the goal of the Nazi Party was to get rid of all the Jews in Europe and that there were two opinions about what to do with them. One group suggested that all Jews be rounded up and shipped out of Europe, maybe to Palestine or Madagascar. The other group, including Hitler, wanted to solve the "Jewish problem" by killing the Jews.

As Varian listened to Hanfstaengl, he was stunned. How could one group of people discuss the possibility of annihilating another group of people? It was such a horrible thought that Varian couldn't quite believe it. Yet he had witnessed the brutality of average Germans toward average Jews the day before. Right away, Varian wrote an article detailing this violence; it appeared in *The New York Times* the next day, July 17, 1935.

At the time, few people outside Germany understood the lengths to which Hitler was willing to go. Ever since he had come to power, Hitler had been steadily working toward taking away the rights of Jews in Germany.

Hitler believed in a racist theory that Germans belonged to a so-called Aryan race. In ancient times, Aryans were people who settled in northern India and spoke a language that became known as Indo-European. In the mid-1800s, Joseph-Arthur, comte de Gobineau, a wealthy Frenchman, wrote a book called *Essay on the Inequality of Human Races*. In it Gobineau suggested that the white race, which he referred to as the Aryan race, was superior to all others. Gobineau's ideas later influenced Houston Stewart Chamberlain, an Englishman with great admiration for Germany. In 1899 Chamberlain's book *The Foundations of the Nineteenth Century* was published. He wrote that all positive influences in Europe came from "Aryans," all negative ones from other races, especially the Jews. Many people believe that Adolf Hitler was inspired by Chamberlain's views. Hitler was convinced that Germans were Aryans, making up a "master race" of Caucasian, non-Jewish people.

When Varian went back home to New York City, he and his wife, Eileen, closely followed the news from Nazi Germany. In September 1935, only a few weeks after Varian returned from Berlin, Germany passed the Nuremberg Laws. These laws took away the civil rights of Jewish people who lived in Germany. It didn't matter to Hitler that the families of these Jewish German citizens had lived there for centuries, or that many Jewish men were war veterans who'd fought for Germany during World War I. What mattered to Hitler was that they were Jews.

The Nuremberg Laws dictated that a "Jew" was anyone who had three or four Jewish grandparents. Suddenly all people considered Jewish were stripped of their German citizenship and segregated from other German citizens. From that point on, it was illegal for a Jew to marry a non-Jewish German. Jews were not permitted to display the German flag, own land, use the legal system, have national health in-

During a boycott of Jewish stores, these S.A. men block an entrance and carry a sign that says: "Germans, defend yourselves against the Jewish atrocity propaganda—buy only at German shops!"

S.A. and university students publicly burned books considered "un-German" on May 10, 1933, in Berlin. Similar burnings took place in other cities.

surance, serve in the military, or own a radio. Jews were forced out of their jobs as newspaper editors, doctors, and lawyers. Jewish teachers could not teach non-Jewish children. Jewish students could not attend a non-Jewish school. Jewish stores were boycotted by Germans. Books written by Jewish authors were publicly burned.

Taking away their rights was only the first phase of Hitler's plan to destroy Jews everywhere. Yet the Jews weren't the only group of people Hitler considered inferior. He intended to wipe out Gypsies, homosexuals, Freemasons (members of a secret society frequently opposed by organized religion), Jehovah's Witnesses (a religious sect who refused to vote, salute, or join the army), and disabled people as well. With Germany's army and air force trained to carry out his orders without hesitation, Hitler had the power to destroy countless people.

Hitler also wanted military domination over as much of Europe as possible. In 1938 Germany took over Austria and seized Czechoslovakia. The next year, with Germany's invasion of Poland, World War II began. In 1940 the Nazis invaded Denmark, Norway, Luxembourg, the Netherlands, Belgium, and France. All countries that came under Hitler's control were bound by Germany's anti-Semitic Nuremberg Laws. As each country fell to Hitler, its Jewish citizens went from being a free and important part of society to having no rights at all. Nazi brutality was displayed again and again as German soldiers humiliated Jews on the streets of Europe.

Those who opposed Hitler and his Nazi Party became known as anti-Nazis. As Hitler's army took over a new country, the secret state police, the Geheime Staatspolizei, known as the Gestapo, moved in. The Gestapo would hunt down and kill every anti-Nazi they could find, including former government leaders, writers, artists, and scientists, as well as average citizens.

When the German army occupied a country, many Jews and anti-Nazis ran for their lives. They became refugees, people who flee to another country for safety. The refugees took with them only what they could carry in their hands, leaving behind all the material possessions they had accumulated in a lifetime.

Before France fell to the

Nazi soldiers delighted in humiliating Jews in every country they conquered. Here a German Nazi laughs at a Polish man with his daughter.

Adolf Hitler and Heinrich Himmler, head of the S.S. and of the Gestapo, review German troops during the Reich Party Day parade in Nuremberg, September 1938.

Germans, refugees from other countries headed there. In the past, France had always welcomed and protected refugees. The capital city, Paris, located in the northern part of the country, overflowed with them.

Varian Fry and all the rest of America listened to news reports as Nazi Germany methodically vanquished the European continent. At this time the United States was not involved in the war. America wouldn't enter the war until the empire of Japan, an ally of Germany, bombed Pearl Harbor on December 7, 1941.

In June 1940 the German army defeated the French. While the Nazis made their way toward Paris, the refugees who had gathered there had to run for their lives again. They were joined by French citizens who also wanted to get away before the Germans arrived. Many of the refugees headed for Marseilles, a busy port city on

After the German army defeated the French, Hitler toured Paris and, on June 23, 1940, posed before the Eiffel Tower. At his right stands Albert Speer, his architect and minister of war production.

the Mediterranean Sea. It was as far from the German army as they could get. Countless people jammed the roads, traveling south through the French countryside in cars and wagons, on bicycles and on foot. Occasionally Nazi airplanes would fly over and shoot at the crowds.

When the victorious Germans arrived in the capital of France, their soldiers marched down the famous street the Champs-Elysées toward the Arc de Triomphe, a monument built to honor the victories of France under Emperor Napoleon I. Hitler posed for photographs with the Eiffel Tower in the background.

Now that they controlled France, the Germans set up a center of government in the city of Vichy (VEE-SHEE). This new system was known as the Vichy government, a network of Frenchmen who collaborated with the Germans and did exactly as they were told. The official leader of the Vichy administration was eighty-four-year-old Philippe Pétain. On June 22, 1940, on behalf of the new Vichy government, Pétain signed an armistice agreement, a truce with the Germans.

Varian had then been working for three years as an author and editor of political books at the Foreign Policy Association's Headline Books in New York. He was alarmed when he read Article 19 of the armistice agreement, which said:

The French Government is obliged to surrender upon demand all Germans named by the German Government in France, as well as in French possessions, Colonies, Protectorate Territories and Mandates.

The French Government binds itself to prevent removal of German war and civil prisoners from France into French possessions or into foreign countries.

Article 19 was phrased politely, but Varian understood what the "surrender upon demand" section meant. The Vichy government agreed to turn over to the Germans anyone in France for whom the Nazis asked. Vichy also agreed to prevent prisoners from leaving France. By prisoners, the Germans meant anyone they wanted to arrest, including Jews and political enemies of Hitler. In effect, Article 19 empowered the Vichy government to keep all of Germany's enemies in France until it was convenient for the Nazis to have them arrested by the Vichy police and delivered to the Germans.

When Varian read the details of Article 19, he remembered what Ernst Hanfstaengl had said five years before. Hanfstaengl had spoken about a Nazi plan to kill Jews. Back then it had been hard for Varian to believe such a plan could be real. But now he had no doubt that Hitler intended to kill every Jew he could get his hands on. Article 19 trapped refugees in France between the German army and the Mediterranean Sea.

And the Germans were coming for them.

[Preparation]

ON JUNE 25, 1940, JUST THREE DAYS AFTER THE French-German armistice was signed, an organization called the American Friends of German Freedom held a luncheon. Varian Fry attended, along with about two hundred other concerned citizens who were leaders in education, religion, the media, and the arts. They met at the Commodore Hotel in New York City to discuss the situation and collect money to help the refugees. These Americans realized that some of the people trapped in France were world-famous writers, painters, sculptors, musicians, scientists, and doctors. If they were not rescued, they would face certain death at the hands of the Nazis. Varian and others were determined not to let this happen.

By the end of the luncheon, three thousand dollars had been donated and a new organization had been formed called the Emergency Rescue Committee (ERC). This committee would have one purpose: to help certain well-known refugees escape France.

The refugees needed a place to go. Each had to find a country that would allow him or her to immigrate. Varian wrote the President of the United States, Franklin D. Roosevelt, to ask him to allow the refugees to come to America. He got a response dated July 8, 1940, from the First Lady, Eleanor Roosevelt: "The President has seen your letter of June 27. He will try to get the cooperation of the South American countries in giving asylum to the political refugees."

Only three weeks after the ERC was created, the committee settled into an office in the Chanin Building, across from Grand Central Terminal in New York City. Dr. Frank Kingdon, a prominent Methodist minister, was named the chairman. Harold Oram, a professional fund-raiser, raised money to support the efforts of the committee. Right away, the ERC had to settle two issues: first, to decide which refugees it wanted to help get out of France; second, to find someone willing to go to France to arrange their escape.

Compiling lists of refugees was the easy part. Leaders from the Museum of Modern Art and the New School for Social Research named prominent people who were in danger. These totaled approximately two hundred men and women, both Jews and non-Jews, who were known in the worlds of art, music, politics, and science. The list included:

Marc Chagall, a Russian-born artist famous for his whimsical scenes using vivid colors, often depicting Jewish folkloric themes.

Max Ernst, a German Surrealist artist who was part of the Dada movement of modern art, which rejected traditional art styles.

Jacques Lipchitz, a Russian-born sculptor influenced by Cubism and known for his large sculptures.

Pablo Picasso, a famous Spanish artist who was one of the co-creators of Cubism, a style of modern art with a fragmented look.

Henri Matisse, a world-famous French painter whose art was considered degenerate by the Nazis.

Franz Werfel, a writer born in Czechoslovakia, famous for his 1933 book *The Forty Days of Musa Dagh*. This book, about the mass murder of Armenians in 1915, was one of thousands publicly burned in Germany.

Lion Feuchtwanger, a world-famous novelist who had been exiled from his native Germany. In 1933 Feuchtwanger published a novel entitled *The Oppermanns* about a German-Jewish family during Hitler's rise to power. The fictional events in the novel turned out to be unbelievably close to actual events. Copies of all Feuchtwanger books published before 1933 were publicly burned on May 10 of that year.

Konrad Heiden, a German writer wanted by the Nazis for his unflattering book *Hitler: A Biography*.

Hertha Pauli, an Austrian anti-Nazi who wrote a biographical novel about the peace activist Bertha von Suttner entitled *Nur eine Frau* (*Only One Woman*), which was banned by the Nazis. She had to flee Austria when the Nazis took over her country.

Otto Meyerhof, a German biochemist who had been awarded a Nobel Prize in 1922 for his work studying the chemistry of muscles.

Heinrich Mann, the older brother of the novelist Thomas Mann and himself a well-known German novelist who also wrote political essays warning the German people about the growing danger from the Nazis. When Hitler came to power, Heinrich Mann was exiled from Germany. His books, too, had been burned on May 10, 1933.

Walter Mehring, a famous German writer who lived in Berlin and composed satirical songs and poems about the Nazis. When they gained control of Germany, Mehring became a wanted man. All of his works were burned on May 10, 1933.

Hans Sahl, a popular German-Jewish poet, playwright, novelist, and film critic who had lived in Berlin until forced to flee.

André Gide, a well-known French writer who was an anti-Nazi. His books were burned on May 10, 1933.

Wanda Landowska, from Poland, a famous harpsichordist who inspired new interest in an instrument that had been around for several centuries. She was one of the greatest players of the harpsichord, and first performed on it in public in 1903.

Erich Itor Kahn, born in Germany to a Russian-Jewish father and a German mother, a classical concert pianist and composer.

Camilla Koffler, from Austria, a photographer professionally called Ylla, best known for her pictures of animals.

❋❋❋

The second task of the newly formed Emergency Rescue Committee—identifying someone to go to France to help get the refugees out—proved that finding a representative was more difficult than the committee had imagined. The right man needed to be able to speak some French and be willing to travel to Nazi-controlled France, where the ERC would make arrangements to snatch certain refugees out of the clutches of Hitler's Gestapo.

Varian Fry volunteered to go. His main qualifications were that he could speak French and some German, and he had traveled in Europe during his college days.

Varian told the ERC, however, "I'm not right for the job. All I know about being a secret agent, or trying to outsmart the Gestapo, is what I've seen in the movies. But if you can't find anyone else, I'll go."

Varian was willing to accept this responsibility for several reasons. First, he believed in freedom and democracy and was concerned when he saw one European country after another fall under the control of a ruthless dictator. Second, it would give him the chance to meet Marc Chagall, Max Ernst, Jacques Lipchitz, Franz

Werfel, Lion Feuchtwanger, Wanda Landowska, and Erich Itor Kahn, all of whose work he had long admired. Varian wrote, "I felt a deep love for these people and a gratitude for the many hours of happiness their books and pictures and music had given me. Now they were in danger. It was my duty to help them, just as they—without knowing it—had often helped me in the past."

Finally, Varian believed that if the refugees did not escape Hitler, they would be killed. Because of what he'd seen in Berlin and the conversation he'd had with Ernst Hanfstaengl, he was one of the few Americans at the time who truly understood what would happen.

Even after Varian offered to go to France, the leaders of the Emergency Rescue Committee continued looking for someone more qualified for the job. After about ten days, the ERC members realized they should not waste any more time getting help to the refugees. Varian Fry was their only choice. They called him in to the office around the middle of July and said, "You're it . . . Get ready to leave at once." When all arrangements had been made, Varian was scheduled to leave for France on August 4, 1940, and return August 29.

How Varian informed his wife and parents, and what they thought of his decision to go to France, is not known. But when he told his friends, some of them advised him not to do it. They thought it was foolish and warned him that he might not come back alive. But it didn't matter what anyone said. Varian had decided to go to Marseilles.

Now Varian had to prepare for the trip. He arranged a month's leave of absence from his job. He also bought a few things he might need in Marseilles, including a shirt from Brooks Brothers.

Varian renewed his passport, which proved he was an American citizen. But he also needed a French visa to enable him to enter France. However, there was a problem with getting this visa, since the Germans were in control and did not allow any Americans except diplomats or relief workers to enter the country. Varian was neither.

In order to get a visa, Varian had to have proof that he would be traveling to France to help people in need. The International Young Men's Christian Association (YMCA), a well-known organization already working in France, wrote a letter claiming it was sending Varian as a relief worker. Both Varian and the YMCA understood he would never actually work for that organization. The letter was intended only to get Varian into France. Once there, he would go about the business of the Emergency Rescue Committee. Because of the YMCA's letter, Varian was issued a French visa.

On the day before Varian left, the Emergency Rescue Committee sent him a letter outlining the duties of the job as they had discussed it. Part of the letter said:

> the Committee realizes that your personal judgment must, under the circumstances existing, play a large part in the success or failure of your efforts on our behalf, and accordingly understands that you are to have a reasonable latitude as to ways and means of carrying out our wishes.

The ERC wanted Varian to accomplish three goals. The first was to report how the work of rescuing the refugees should be carried out. The second was "to attempt to locate, and to aid with counsel and money as directed, certain individuals whom this Committee will specify, so that they may reach Lisbon or Casablanca and thereby be in a better position to be transported to this continent." The third was to find people in France and Portugal who could work on behalf of the refugees after Varian returned.

On August 4 Eileen Fry and a few friends went with Varian to La-

Guardia Airport to say goodbye. Varian boarded the luxurious Pan American Dixie Clipper, a huge "flying boat" designed to take off and land in the water. He had a ticket for a return flight less than a month later. His pockets were stuffed with lists of men and women he had been sent to help. The three thousand dollars that had been collected by the ERC to help the refugees was taped to Varian's leg, hidden under his pants.

Anyone looking at thirty-two-year-old Varian during the transatlantic flight from New York to Lisbon, Portugal, would never have believed he was an agent on a secret mission to defy Adolf Hitler. He certainly didn't look the part. He was thin, and his big horn-rimmed eyeglasses gave him a bookish look, as if he spent long hours studying in the library.

On the surface, it seemed that nothing in the life of Varian Mackey Fry had prepared him for what lay ahead. He was born on October 15, 1907, and grew up in Ridgewood, New Jersey. He was a pampered only child, but he didn't see either of his parents much. Arthur Fry, his father, was a quiet man who worked at a stock brokerage firm in New York City. The long commute into the city and back each day meant that by the time his father got home from work, little Varian was already in bed. His mother, Lilian Fry, a former schoolteacher, had repeated nervous breakdowns. Several times Varian watched as his mother was taken from their home to be admitted to the hospital for treatment. She would be gone for months at a time. Lilian's two unmarried sisters, Laura and Florence Mackey, had lived with the Frys ever since Lilian and Arthur married. So with his parents often away, Varian was cared for by his aunts.

The happiest times of Varian's childhood were his twice-a-year visits with his grandfather Charles Fry. Varian adored the kindhearted man, whose life was an example of his Christian faith, shown in the love he felt for those less fortunate. Charles Fry was the superintendent of the Children's Summer Home in Brooklyn, run by the Children's Aid Society. This organization was dedicated to rescuing abandoned and orphaned children from the streets of New York City. Children from the slums of the city could have a one-week vacation at the Children's Summer Home in the country. That part of Brooklyn was then an almost rural area, complete with cows.

Since Varian was an only child in a household of four adults, he usually got his way. But if things didn't go as he wanted them to, his temper would flare up. His father wrote a poem about Varian's behavior:

This Goop bounces on the bed,
First on his feet, then on his head.
His mother tells him to get dressed,
For mothers always know what's best.
But he won't do as he's told.
He'll be a Goop and catches cold.
Don't be a Goop.

This Goop is Varian Mackey Fry.
Just watch him make his oatmeal fly.
It's on the cloth, it's on the floor,
It's even spattered on the door.
A boy of six is much too big
To eat his breakfast like a pig.
Don't be a Goop.

As he grew up, it was clear that Varian was intelligent. He excelled in music and his schoolwork—at least when he was interested

Ten-year-old Varian rescued this bird, a cedar waxwing, from the clutches of a cat.

in the subject. Varian was as stubborn as he was smart, which meant he could accomplish anything he set out to do. But his strong will, mixed with occasional bursts of a bad temper, meant that sometimes he had trouble making friends—and trouble keeping them. He didn't like team sports; instead he preferred spending time alone watching birds.

Varian was also a bit of an actor. He frequently faked being sick so he could stay home from school, especially when it was raining. And he always got away with it. If his mother was home, she would read aloud to him. This instilled in him a deep love for reading and books.

When Varian was thirteen, his beloved grandfather Charles Fry died. The next year Varian went to live at Hotchkiss, a boys' boarding school in Lakeville, Connecticut. He didn't like to follow the rules. And he didn't like it when an authority figure told him what to do. At Hotchkiss, Varian participated in school pranks such as throwing oranges and using a mirror to flash sunshine around the classroom. He even got into a fight or two. When he was in trouble with the principal, he wrote letters back home to his father that were full of remorse for what he had done. But he also complained that he had been singled out unfairly.

Varian had always hated his name. He thought it sounded like a

Varian, around twelve years old, with his Dandie Dinmont terrier.

girl's. While he was at Hotchkiss, Varian decided he wanted his schoolmates and family to call him Tommy. He even signed "Tommy" on his letters home. But no one would cooperate with him, so he eventually gave it up.

Early on, Varian was un-afraid to stand up for what he believed in. James Joyce's novel *Ulysses*, published in 1922, was banned from the United States because many people considered it ob-scene. Somehow Varian got a copy of the book. He enjoyed it so much that he shared it with a group of friends who would gather to listen to Varian read it aloud. Together, they tried to overturn the ban on the book, but they were not successful. In December of 1933, about ten years after Varian's efforts at Hotchkiss, a federal court judge lifted the ban against *Ulysses*, which allowed the book to be published in the United States.

In December 1924, when he was a junior in high school, Var-ian refused to participate in a long-standing hazing tradition at Hotchkiss. Each year, as a sort of rite of passage, the seniors required the juniors to cross a room hand over hand while hanging from a hot overhead pipe. Varian thought it was ridiculous.

No one had ever before resisted, and the entire student body and faculty pressured Varian to submit to the ritual. The more they tried to persuade him, the more adamant he became. When the school administration insisted that he participate, Varian resigned from the school rather than back down. His father supported his decision.

Varian's father then enrolled him at the Taft School in Connecticut, where he finished his junior year. But Varian was unable to make friends and was unhappy there. In the fall of 1925 he began his senior year closer to home at Riverdale Country School in the Bronx, New York City. He lived at home through the school year, driving back and forth in a Packard convertible his father had bought for him. But Varian's last year in high school wasn't a happy one either.

In the fall of 1926 Varian began college at Harvard in Cambridge, Massachusetts. He moved into Gore Hall, a freshman dormitory with a view of the Charles River, where crew teams practiced rowing their long, thin boats. He became friends with another freshman named Lincoln Kirstein. Both were considered outsiders at Harvard: Lincoln because he was Jewish, Varian because his family was not as wealthy as those of the other students.

Since Lincoln and Varian each had a deep love of literature, they sought editorial positions at *The Harvard Advocate*, a student literary journal. Both were rejected. So together they decided to create their own literary journal, *Hound & Horn*. It was funded by Lincoln's father. The first issue was published in the spring of 1927. The journal was a hit, and suddenly Varian and Lincoln became popular. A couple of years later, apparently at Lincoln's insistence, two other students joined them as editors. Because Varian did not approve of these additions to the staff, in 1929 he resigned from the journal he'd cofounded. Still, he continued his friendship with Lincoln while at Harvard.

Later in life, Lincoln Kirstein, one of the founders of the New York City Ballet, wrote a book called *Mosaic: Memoirs*. In it he recalled that Varian felt he was smarter than other people.

Varian traveled to Europe for the first time during the summer before his junior year at Harvard. He sailed on the ship SS *Sinaia*. He visited many places, including Portugal, northern France, Greece, and Turkey. Varian so enjoyed the Greek islands that when he returned to school he decided to concentrate his studies on the classic Greek and Roman cultures and languages.

Two completely different sides of Varian's personality were evident during his days at Harvard. At times he was mature and serious. But at other times, according to a biography about Varian entitled *A Hero of Our Own*, by Sheila Isenberg, he drove around recklessly in his Packard convertible, pulled college pranks, and attended wild parties at which he drank too much. Although Varian had been on probation before, one prank got him into a lot of trouble during the summer before his senior year. He was expelled from Harvard after putting a stolen FOR SALE sign on the university president's lawn.

Two people pleaded with the Harvard administration to give Varian another chance. Because of their intervention, Harvard allowed Varian to return—but only if he repeated his entire junior year. One of these people was a professor, William C. Greene. The other was a friend of Varian's named Eileen Avery Hughes, whom he had met through Lincoln Kirstein. She worked as a magazine editor at *The Atlantic Monthly*, a well-respected magazine in Boston.

Eileen was six years older than Varian. Although she was a mature career woman and he was an immature college student, they fell in love. During Varian's last two years at Harvard, Eileen was a stabilizing influence. She looked out for Varian, and when his party-animal lifestyle caused problems, she would find a way to get him out of trouble.

At last, in May 1931, Varian graduated from Harvard with a bachelor of arts degree. Eileen and Varian married soon after, on June 2. Eileen was twenty-nine, and Varian was twenty-three. They moved to New York City to begin their life together. America was then in the grip of the Great Depression, and like everyone else, the newlyweds had little money. Eileen got a job at *Time* as a researcher. Varian found a part-time job at *Consumers' Research* magazine. He also taught Latin at a school in New York City.

During the next two years, Varian became more and more interested in political and social issues. Aware of how difficult it was for a college graduate to get a good job during the Depression, he joined the Association of Unemployed College Alumni, founded by Joseph P. Lash. In 1933, the same year that Adolf Hitler became Chancellor of Germany, Varian and Lash went to Washington, D.C., to raise awareness of the shortage of jobs for college graduates. Both were supporters of the new President of the United States, Franklin D. Roosevelt, who had been in office only a few months. Varian and Lash were allowed to meet with President Roosevelt to discuss their concerns. Joseph P. Lash would eventually write several biographies about the Roosevelts.

Later in 1933 Varian got a job at *The Scholastic* magazine. He also began studying political science at Columbia University. Eileen found a good job teaching English at a private girls' school.

A couple of years later, Varian became editor of *The Living Age*, a magazine that focused on foreign issues. It was this role that prompted him to take a three-month-long trip in 1935 to see for himself what was happening to Jews in Germany.

Now, five years after he'd witnessed the riot, he was in a plane crossing the Atlantic Ocean, on his way to Marseilles, France. He could not forget what he'd seen in Berlin. He could still recall the tune and the words the Germans had chanted:

When Jewish blood spurts from the knife,
Then everything will be fine again.

That day Varian had been powerless to help any of the Jewish people who were mistreated. Since then Hitler had grown more powerful. Now Varian was going back to Europe, this time with hidden lists and money. He planned to defy Hitler by rescuing Jewish refugees.

But how?

[Papers]

VARIAN ARRIVED EXHAUSTED ON AUGUST 5, 1940, AFTER a thirty-six-hour trip to Lisbon, Portugal. He planned to rest there awhile before going on to Marseilles, France. He also wanted to find out as much as possible about the refugee situation. Varian met with leaders of other relief organizations, such as the Unitarian Service Committee, that were already providing aid to refugees. He also met with various consuls, government officials who represent citizens of their countries while they are living or traveling in foreign nations.

Varian learned that refugees were trying to get from Marseilles to Lisbon because Portugal was one of the few remaining countries from which a refugee could leave Europe. The route from France to Portugal included travel through Spain, which, under the dictatorship of Francisco Franco, was sympathetic to the Hitler regime. Since Portugal and Spain didn't fight for or against the Nazis, they were considered neutral countries during World War II.

Varian learned that in war-torn Europe, having the right papers was crucial. At any time an official such as a policeman or a border guard could check a refugee's papers to see if they were "in order."

Papers were considered in order if they included all the necessary documents and none was out of date. An individual whose papers were not in order could be arrested immediately.

To travel legally from France to Lisbon, Portugal, a refugee needed the following:

1. A passport, a document issued by the government of his or her home country containing personal information and a photograph. This was required to travel from one country to another, and to obtain all the rest of the documents.

2. A safe-conduct pass, or transit visa, for France, a document from the Vichy government allowing the refugee to travel within the country.

3. A French exit visa, a document from the Vichy government allowing the refugee to leave France.

4. A travel visa for Spain, a document from the Spanish government allowing the refugee to enter Spain.

5. A transit visa from Spain, a document from the Spanish government allowing the refugee to travel through Spain. A transit visa was given with the understanding that the refugees would pass through the country on their way to somewhere else.

6. A travel visa for Portugal, a document from the Portuguese government allowing a refugee to enter Portugal.

7. A transit visa from Portugal, a document from the Portuguese government allowing the refugee to travel through Portugal.

8. A travel visa from some other country—any other country besides Portugal—giving the refugee permission to enter that country. Even a refugee who made it as far as Lisbon couldn't board a ship and leave Europe without a visa to go somewhere else.

For refugees in Marseilles who were trying to get out of Europe, the process of gathering all the documents was difficult and time-consuming. They had to fill out applications for documents from France, Spain, Portugal, and a host country. All applications for French safe-conduct visas and exit visas were processed in an office run by the Vichy government. Names of the refugees were checked against a list of people wanted by the Gestapo. If a refugee's name was on the Gestapo's list, the application to travel through and leave France would be denied. If it was accepted, the refugee then applied at the Spanish Consulate for the documents to travel through Spain, then at the Portuguese Consulate for the documents to travel through Portugal. And finally the refugee applied for a visa at the consulate of each and every country possible, in hopes of being given permission to enter any country in the world that was not controlled by Adolf Hitler. Although most refugees hoped they could go to the United States of America, they were willing to go anywhere.

As Varian learned what the refugees needed to get safely out of Europe, he also learned that even when a person was granted a document, his or her problems were far from over. Each document had an expiration date. The Portuguese transit visa was good for one month and the Spanish transit visa for two weeks. Sometimes this meant that as a refugee waited to get the last document needed, the date on another document would expire—and the application process for that one had to be started over again.

It was hard enough for one refugee to have all the documents at the same time. The situation grew more complicated if the refugee had a family, since each person in the family needed every document.

All refugees were after the same goal: gathering the documents necessary to leave Europe. But Jewish refugees who had been born in Germany had an additional complication. None of them had the most critical document, a passport. The Nuremberg Laws of 1935 declared that Jews were no longer citizens of Germany. Therefore every German Jew was "stateless" and did not have a passport. Without a passport, a refugee could not obtain any other foreign documents required to legally flee Europe.

When Varian had learned all he could in Lisbon about the needs of the refugees, he traveled by plane to Barcelona, Spain. From there he caught a train that would take him the rest of the way to Marseilles. After crossing the border between Spain and France, the train stopped at each small town along the French coast. More and more passengers boarded as it chugged its way toward the city.

On August 15, 1940, Varian's train pulled into Gare Saint-Charles, the railroad station in Marseilles. The hum of the French language surrounded Varian as the huge crowd surged toward the police inspectors' checkpoint. A line formed so that the papers for each and every passenger could be checked. Now that the Nazis ruled France, even French people had to have a safe-conduct pass in order to travel within their own country. It was immediately clear to Varian that he'd left in America the freedom to go anywhere he wanted without permission, without questions, without papers.

The police were making sure that everyone had a safe-conduct pass and that all foreigners had a valid passport. Anyone without the proper documents would be immediately arrested.

When it was Varian's turn, he handed the policeman his passport.

In his book *Assignment: Rescue*, Varian wrote about his encounter with this Vichy policeman:

"Aha, an American," he said in a gravel-rough voice.

"Yes," I said, trying to keep my voice calm.

"Marseilles is like your New York City at rush hour, eh?" he said, smiling.

I smiled back. "Quite a mob," I said.

"Refugees. Pouring down from the north," he said. "We would like to pour them back. But the Boches [Germans] have occupied Paris. So the refugees all run to Marseilles to hide, or maybe sneak across the border. But they won't escape. Sooner or later we arrest all the illegal ones." He smiled again.

"Too bad for them," I said.

"Too bad for them; too bad for us!" He gave me my passport. "Enjoy your stay in our country," he said. "But why you visit us at this unsettled time, I don't know."

His eyes narrowed, and I thought he looked at me suspiciously. But as I went out through the gate, I decided it was my imagination. He knew nothing of the lists in my pockets, nor did he know I had come to smuggle out of France the people whose names were on those lists.

The reality of what he was doing hit Varian. He was in Nazi-controlled France talking to a Vichy policeman who had the authority to arrest him. Some of the people on his lists of names were considered personal enemies of Adolf Hitler. And taped to his leg he had three thousand dollars that he planned to use to smuggle those people out of France.

It was already hot by the time Varian got outside the station that morning. Across the street from the station was the white marble staircase that led down to the tree-lined Boulevard d'Athènes. Varian stopped at the top of the steps and looked out over Marseilles. In the distance, he could see mountains and the Notre-Dame de la Garde (Our Lady of the Guard) Catholic Basilica, which perched on the crest of the hill overlooking the entire city.

Varian made his way down the 104 steps, past the ornate statues and lampposts that lined the magnificent staircase. Just a block down from the bottom of the stairs and to the right, he couldn't miss the huge sign advertising the hotel where he intended to stay, the Splendide.

He arrived to find that the Splendide had no vacancies. Varian left his name and asked the clerk to save a room for him when one became available. He checked into a hotel right across from the train station that he thought smelled like "drains and garlic."

Varian locked the door to his room. He emptied his pockets and spread the lists on the nightstand. He stared down at two hundred or so names. Each represented a person whose life was in danger. In many cases, the people on the list had families who must also be rescued.

He had come to get as many of these people as possible out of France. He suspected there would be a brief period before the Gestapo was organized enough in the South of France to start arresting them. Varian had addresses for only a few refugees, but it was impossible to know if they were still at those locations. The only refugee he knew he could find for sure was Franz Werfel. As for the rest, Varian wondered how he would find them in a city teeming with hundreds of thousands of refugees from all over Europe. And what would he do with them if he found them? How could he get them out of France safely?

He decided to visit the American Consulate in Marseilles. He walked through the massive front door to the offices downtown and approached the receptionist's desk. Varian asked her if he could speak to the consul about visas. She explained that the visa department was located away from the center of town, in Montredon, and that he would need to take a trolley to get there. She handed him a piece of paper with the address written on it.

The blue-and-cream-colored trolley already had a load of passengers, but Varian managed to squeeze in anyway. The trolley rattled its way through the city. When it made a stop, Varian was surprised to hear that instead of the usual clanking bell, it blew a foghorn. He thought it made a sad sound. Varian took in the sights of the city where he planned to spend the next two weeks. Occasionally he caught the mouth-watering scent of freshly baked bread as people hurried home carrying long, unwrapped loaves of French bread in their arms.

People were everywhere, like ants swarming around a huge anthill. The city was full of French soldiers who had been demobilized after the Germans defeated them. The French army had included many different types of soldiers, both from France and from its colonies and protectorates in North Africa such as Morocco, Tunisia, and Algeria. Riding through the city, Varian saw the colorful uniforms of the various branches of the military. The members of the French Foreign Legion wore white hats; the men of the army's armored battalion wore berets low over the ears; the soldiers from Morocco wore red fezzes; those from the West African country of Senegal wore turbans wrapped around their heads and held in place by a star.

In addition to the soldiers and the citizens of Marseilles, there were countless refugees from all over Europe. Varian thought that most of the people on the trolley must be refugees. He could see in their eyes a sort of "bewildered" look. Their clothes confirmed what he suspected. The refugees looked as if they'd been wearing the same clothes for weeks on end—and they had been.

The trolley passed gray limestone hills, date palms, and pine trees, until the unmistakable smell of fish and sea filled the air. After a sharp left turn, the trolley continued down the coast, past beach houses crammed next to each other. The heat of the August afternoon combined with the rocking motion of the trolley made Varian sleepy.

When the trolley stopped, Varian saw the visa division of the American Consulate. It was located on an estate at the end of a driveway lined on both sides with plane trees, which were common in France. The whole group of refugees surged together toward the house. Varian let the crowd go on ahead while he cooled off under the shade of the outstretched branches. He could hear the surf as it lapped upon the nearby beach, and the soft trickle of water that ran down the ditches toward the sea.

As Varian walked up the drive and neared the huge brick house, he realized that the crowd of refugees had filled up the inside of the house and overflowed onto the front porch. Hertha Pauli, a refugee from Austria, wrote in her book *Break of Time* that the visa division of the American Consulate in Montredon looked like a castle. Although she and the other refugees who gathered there wanted to speak to the American consul, "the admission we sought was not to the castle. The castle stood for a dream. In our dreams, in the dreams of all these fugitives from the ever-widening range of Hitler's power, the white steps in the outskirts of Marseilles led to the Promised

Land." All refugees who went to the castle hoped the United States government would give them a visa. In the Promised Land of America, they would not need to fear the Nazis. In America they would be safe.

If only they could get there.

Varian, secure in the knowledge that he was an American citizen, climbed the white marble steps, walked past the refugees, and entered the front door into the main hall.

"What do you mean, trying to get ahead of the others? . . . Go back to your place and wait your turn," a man told him in French.

Varian explained that he was an American who was there to see the consul about refugee visas. When the man heard that Varian was a U.S. citizen, he changed his attitude and his language. In English, he assured Varian that he would take his business card to the consul, and led him into an office to wait.

Varian sat in the office filled with mahogany desks and filing cabinets. From the bay windows, he looked out over the Château Pastré, the beautiful mansion next door whose many windows were bordered by white shutters. The massive house was surrounded by trees and a manicured lawn. Varian could see the sparkling blue sea in front of it and the mountains behind it. The peace and quiet of the scene outside contrasted sharply with the chaos inside, where the sound of refugees speaking both German and French mingled into a constant buzz.

A few minutes later, another man found Varian and ordered him back to the waiting room. After sitting there for two hours, Varian gave up and left. He had gotten a taste of how refugees were treated.

Only hours after his attempt to see the American consul, Varian met with the first of the refugees on his list, Franz Werfel and his wife, Alma. Franz Werfel was a well-known Jewish writer. Alma

Mahler Werfel was known as an inspiration for famous men. Several musicians, writers, and artists had been in love with her through the years. Her first husband was the composer Gustav Mahler. After his death, the painter Oskar Kokoschka fell in love with her and painted her portrait several times. Her second husband was the architect Walter Gropius. Franz Werfel was Alma's third husband.

While in Lisbon, Varian had met Franz Werfel's sister. She'd told Varian the name of the hotel where the Werfels were staying. She also told him they were registered under the name of Gustav Mahler, who had been dead for almost thirty years.

When Varian finally met the pale, short, and stocky Franz Werfel, he thought of a "half-filled sack of flour." He noticed that Werfel's hair was thin on top of his head, where it started growing about halfway back. Alma, a dark-haired beauty in her youth, was eleven years older than her husband.

Speaking English with a heavy Austrian accent, Franz Werfel told Varian about the difficulties they'd experienced. They had fled from their home in Austria to Paris, and from Paris had escaped to Lourdes, and from Lourdes to Marseilles. They had American visas in their possession. But they did not have French exit visas, which would allow them to leave France legally. They had applied for the visas, but hadn't heard whether or not they would be granted.

The longer they stayed in Marseilles, the greater was their risk of being discovered and turned over to the Gestapo. Without all their travel documents, the Werfels didn't know what to do next. Should they try to leave France illegally, without an exit visa? What if they were caught and arrested?

"You must save us, Mr. Fry," insisted Franz Werfel.

In her book *And the Bridge Is Love*, Alma Werfel wrote about this meeting with Varian Fry. "Mr. Fry did the job," she said, "but his laconic manner and expressionless face made him appear to be doing it gruffly and grudgingly." She noticed that Varian said very little.

The Werfels didn't realize that on that night, Varian's first in Marseilles, he had no idea how to get them safely out of France. Finally he advised them to stay in their hotel until he could find out more about their chances for escape.

The next day Varian had an informative meeting with Frank Bohn, a representative of the American Federation of Labor. Bohn, Varian had been told in New York, was also secretly working in Marseilles to help refugees escape. However, he was interested in a completely different group of people. Bohn's list included only European labor leaders and political figures.

Varian shared with Bohn his experience at the visa division of the American Consulate, but Bohn assured him that they would have the support of the American vice-consul in Marseilles, Hiram (Harry) Bingham. Then Bohn told Varian that one of the most important people Varian had come to rescue, Lion Feuchtwanger, was actually hiding at Harry Bingham's villa. He explained how Feuchtwanger had gotten there.

Lion Feuchtwanger was on a lecture tour in America in 1933 when the Nazis stripped him of German citizenship. His home in Berlin was searched and his precious library destroyed. When he and his wife, Marta, left the United States, they could not return to Germany. They went to France to start over, to Sanary, a small coastal village near Marseilles.

In May of 1940 the Feuchtwangers and thousands of other Jewish Germans who had fled to France to escape Hitler were forced into French concentration camps. Men and women were not usually allowed to stay together. Lion was originally held in a camp at Les Milles, then sent to Saint-Nicolas, a camp near the city of Nîmes, northwest of Marseilles. Marta, with about ten thousand other women, was sent to a camp called Gurs. Fortunately, Marta had been released that summer. A smart, energetic woman determined to free her husband, she sought help from Harry Bingham.

Conditions in the concentration camps such as the one where Lion Feuchtwanger was imprisoned were horrible. (Later in the war, some concentration camps became death camps, where people were systematically murdered.) The inmates didn't have enough to eat and endured filthy living conditions. Many prisoners got sick, including Feuchtwanger. He became so ill that his friends in the camp wondered if he would survive.

Yet the prisoners at Saint-Nicolas had one privilege: they were al-

Novelist Lion Feuchtwanger (facing camera) while imprisoned in a concentration camp at Les Milles.

lowed to walk to a local swimming hole to wash and swim. Although the men were not guarded, they all knew it was useless to run away. Occasionally, one would walk away and not return. But if he was missing at roll call, the guards searched the countryside until he was found.

One day in mid-August, as Feuchtwanger walked back to camp after a swim, he was intercepted on the road by a woman he knew. She handed him a note. He recognized his wife's handwriting. The note said: "Do exactly as you are told. Do not stop to consider. It is all straightforward and perfectly sure."

Feuchtwanger looked up and saw a waiting car. A man wearing a white suit stepped out. Speaking with an American accent, he told Feuchtwanger to get in. Once Feuchtwanger and the woman were in the car, the driver, Miles Standish, a deputy consul at the American Consulate office in Marseilles, told him to put on the disguise they had brought for him. Without hesitation, Feuchtwanger put on the lightweight woman's coat, headscarf, and ladies' sunglasses. If anyone stopped them for questioning, the small, thin Feuchtwanger would appear to be an old English lady. Standish drove Feuchtwanger to the Marseilles home of Harry Bingham.

Varian was relieved to hear from Bohn that Feuchtwanger and his wife were safe. Now Varian could work on finding a way to get them out of France. Bohn then looked at Varian's lists and told him the whereabouts of a few of the refugees whom he knew.

Bohn explained to Varian that he'd been meeting with refugees in his room at the hotel and suggested that Varian do the same. Later that same day, Varian moved into room 324 at the Hôtel Splendide.

Below Varian's hotel window was the courtyard of a girls' school. At recess, Varian's room was filled with joyful giggles and squeals. But when the girls were not at play, Varian noticed that although the

Because of a gasoline shortage, some people built and attached charcoal burners to power their vehicles. As the charcoal burned, gases were given off, cooled, then routed to the carburetor to run the engine. The benefit was the nice smell of a burning fireplace, which permeated the city.

city was full of people, it was quiet—unnaturally quiet, like the calm before a storm. Since the defeat of the French army about two months before, the French had gone into a period of mourning and had forbidden dancing and playing jazz music.

Now settled in the hotel, Varian immediately wrote letters to the refugees for whom Bohn had given him addresses. He explained to them that he'd just arrived from America and had a message for them. He asked them to come to his hotel to meet with him.

During Varian's first couple of days in Marseilles, he added two new French words to his vocabulary. Everywhere he went, he heard people describing the Marseilles situation as *pagaille*, which means "mess, utter confusion." He had to agree. Although there wasn't a shortage of food—yet—there was a shortage of razor blades, soap, and gasoline. The chaos was illustrated in heart-wrenching notices from refugee families who had gotten separated as they ran from the Germans. Varian read in the newspapers: "Mother seeks baby daughter, age two, lost on the road between Tours and Poitiers in the retreat," and "Generous reward for information leading to the recovery of my son Jacques, age ten, last seen at Bordeaux, June 17th."

The other word Varian learned was *débrouiller. Se débrouiller* means "to look out for yourself."

Varian was ready to begin his work representing the Emergency Rescue Committee. It was legal in Vichy France for foreign organizations to help refugees by giving them money for their basic needs of food, clothing, and shelter. These groups were also free to help refugees seek visas. In addition to the YMCA, whose letter had helped Varian get into France, several other relief organizations were already working in Marseilles, including the American Red Cross, the American Friends Service Committee (a Quaker organization), the Unitarian Service Committee, and HICEM (a Jewish organization).

It was absolutely legal to help refugees survive while they were in France.

It was absolutely illegal to help refugees who did not have all their papers in order to get out of France. But that was exactly what Varian intended to do.

[Choices]

NEWS QUICKLY SPREAD THROUGHOUT MARSEILLES THAT an American had arrived to help some refugees escape. At first no one knew his name. It was whispered that this American had an endless supply of money and visas. A man in Toulouse was selling Varian's name and address. Some refugees dismissed the story as just another rumor. Others suspected it was a trap. All of them hoped it was true.

The day after Varian moved into the Hôtel Splendide, a stream of refugees began to appear at his door. The first to arrive were a small group of young Austrians who had fled their country because their political beliefs put them in danger. All had American visas giving them permission to enter the United States, and visas giving them permission to travel through Spain and Portugal. What the Austrians did not have was French exit visas, giving them permission to leave France. Anyone who left without an exit visa was breaking the law and, if caught, could be arrested and sent to a concentration camp.

The Austrians had already planned their escape from France

without exit visas. They explained to Varian that they would leave Marseilles and travel to Cerbère, more than two hundred miles away. Cerbère was a small town located on the French side of the border between France and Spain, just three miles from Portbou, a small town on the Spanish side. Although only three miles apart, these two towns on the Mediterranean coast were separated by an international border.

In Cerbère, the Austrians would have to avoid the Vichy police. Usually a traveler would change trains at the border to enter Spain, but the Austrians were afraid the police would check their papers and discover they didn't have exit visas. So they planned to walk around the entire area and enter Spain far from any official border crossing.

There was only one problem—going around Cerbère meant they must climb over the Pyrenees Mountains. The mountains of the Pyrenees are a natural border between France and Spain that stretches from the Mediterranean Sea all the way to the Atlantic Ocean.

The Austrians even had a secret map. It showed a path near a cemetery that would give them some protection from being seen by the local police as they left Cerbère. From there they hoped to slip unnoticed up the mountainside. The border between the two countries was indicated by crosses on the map. Arrows showed the best way to avoid the French border patrols.

If the Austrians could climb over the Pyrenees and reach the Spanish side of the mountain range without getting caught by the French police, they would most likely be safe. They believed that the Spanish border guards would not care if they had French exit visas or not. However, the Spanish guards needed to make sure the refugees had transit visas giving them permission to travel through Spain. Then they would get an official Spanish entrance stamp on their passports. If a policeman anywhere in Spain checked their papers and didn't find the entrance stamp, they would be arrested immediately.

Once in Spain with an entrance stamp, the Austrians would go to nearby Portbou and buy train tickets to Lisbon, Portugal. In Lisbon, they could make arrangements to sail on a ship to America because they had visas from the United States giving them permission to enter the country.

The plan, which the Austrians explained in detail to Varian, was complicated and risky—but it was the only way. They were ready to go and had everything they needed except money for train tickets and food. They had come to Varian for this.

Varian gave them what they needed. Grateful, they gave Varian their secret map so that others could follow it. The Austrians had already memorized the safe passage through the Pyrenees and no longer needed it.

After the young men left his room, Varian knew he must hide the valuable map. He looked around for a safe place. The best choice was to stash it behind the mirror attached to the closet door. Carefully Varian loosened the screws holding the mirror and slid the secret map behind it. Then he tightened the screws.

After the Austrians, other refugees came to Varian's door. One, whose name was on one of Varian's original lists, was the writer Hans Sahl. Sahl had escaped from a French concentration camp and made his way to Marseilles. A friend told Sahl about Varian Fry and that his name was on Varian's list. Sahl telephoned Varian at the hotel and was told to come right over. In his book *The Few and the Many*, Sahl wrote about his meeting with Varian:

> When I appeared at the hotel ten minutes later, two German officers
> were standing in the lobby. I walked past them to the elevator, rode

up, and who should open his door but a friendly young man in shirt sleeves who welcomed me in, put his arm around my shoulders, tucked money into my pocket, drew me over to the window, and whispered out of one corner of his mouth, like a rather poor actor playing the part of a plotter: "If you need more, come back again. Meanwhile I'll cable your name to Washington. We'll get you out of here. There are ways. You'll see—oh, there are ways . . ."

Imagine the situation: the borders closed; you're caught in a trap, might be arrested again at any moment; life is as good as over—and suddenly a young American in shirt sleeves is stuffing your pockets full of money, putting his arm around your shoulders, and whispering with the conspiratorial expression of a ham actor: "Oh there are ways to get you out of here," while . . . the tears were streaming down my face, actual tears, big, round, and wet; and that pleasant fellow, a Harvard man incidentally, takes a silk handkerchief from his jacket and says: "Here, have this. Sorry it isn't cleaner." You know, since that day I have loved America.

While waiting for an American visa and a chance to escape France, Hans Sahl helped Varian at the ERC office.

Varian threw himself into the work with all of his energy. Every day more and more refugees heard about Varian Fry. And every day more and more refugees came to Varian's door and told him about the traumatic experiences they'd had. By the end of his first week, a line of refugees had formed in the hall. Most who came were not on the lists Varian had brought with him. But when Varian did meet with a refugee who was on the list, he showed the names to that person to see if he or she knew the whereabouts of any of the others.

The original plan was that Varian would be in Marseilles for about two weeks. It had all sounded so simple when he was in New York, but the reality of the refugee situation was much more complicated than he or the Emergency Rescue Committee had realized. Now that he was in Marseilles, Varian understood that it was impossible to locate the refugees he'd come for and arrange safe passage for them in such a short time.

Each day the line outside his door was so long that Varian realized he needed help. During his second week in Marseilles, instead of preparing to return home, he was preparing to hire a staff to assist him with the paperwork.

The first person who joined Varian was Dr. Albert Hirschman, a twenty-five-year-old German who had completed a doctorate in economics and had been fighting in the French army. He was in real danger from the Germans, not only because he was Jewish, but also because he'd fought with the French against them. When his commanding officer released him from the defeated army, the officer offered to conceal Albert's true identity by issuing his demobilization papers under a false name. Albert got to re-create himself as a French citizen, using a new name and new place of birth. He chose the name Albert Hermant and decided that he had been born to French parents in Philadelphia, Pennsylvania, U.S.A.

Albert, who spoke English with a German accent, was good-natured and grinned frequently, which is why Varian gave him the nickname Beamish. Varian depended on Albert's expertise in areas that involved undercover work.

Next Varian took on Franz von Hildebrand, whom Varian called Franzi. He was a blond-haired, blue-eyed Catholic from Austria. He spoke English as if he were from the upper classes of England— except that he frequently threw in colorful doses of profanity. Since

The false identity card of Dr. Albert Hirschman (Beamish) in the name of Albert Hermant.

he had previous experience running a relief committee in Paris, Varian depended on him to set up the office so that it ran as smoothly as possible.

Refugees continued to arrive at Varian's door and wait patiently to see Varian or one of his team. Then, when letters began to pour in from French concentration camps asking for help, Varian realized he needed a secretary. He hired Lena Fishman to type letters for him. Lena, who was Polish, had been a social worker in Paris. She spoke French, German, English, Spanish, Russian, and Polish. She had the habit of mixing languages together as she talked by saying the first half of a sentence in one language and the second half in another.

One day an American named Miriam Davenport stood in the refugee line for her turn to see Varian. While studying art history at the University of Paris, Miriam had fallen in love with a young man from Yugoslavia. Her fiancé, who had returned to his homeland, was then unable to leave again because he didn't have the proper papers. Miriam had come to Marseilles to obtain the documents she needed to go to Yugoslavia and get him out. However, when Miriam approached Varian, it was on behalf of the German poet Walter

Mehring, who had asked Miriam to speak to Varian for him. Mehring had been questioned by the police the day before and was afraid that if the police saw him again on the street, they would arrest him. In her memoir, *An Unsentimental Education*, Miriam remembered that Varian was dressed in a nice pin-striped suit with good cuff links and shoes. She wrote that he was "a full-blown American 'preppie.' His direct, unblinking regard and cordial, impersonal smile spoke louder than words. 'I am a pleasant enough fellow, my business is above reproach, and I shall not be deterred.' "

Varian soon found out that Miriam spoke excellent French and German, and she knew the location of many of the refugees he was trying to find. He asked her to join his staff. She accepted because she wanted to help the refugees, the majority of whom were Jewish. Later in life, Miriam Davenport gave an in-depth interview to Emmy Award–winning filmmaker Pierre Sauvage for his forthcoming documentary entitled *And Crown Thy Good: Varian Fry in Marseille*. In the interview, Miriam Davenport said: "The Book of Ruth was read to me as a fairy tale when I was a child. And one of the lines in that is more or less, 'Your people are my people.' And I felt very strongly that these people were indeed my people, and that I had to do something about it."

It is interesting that filmmaker Pierre Sauvage's father, Léo, was a journalist who sought help from Varian Fry in Marseilles. Léo Smotriez and his wife, Barbara, were Jews who had changed their last name to the French name of Sauvage in the 1930s. They were among the many refugees whom Varian did not help. Sometime after meeting with Varian, they were advised by a friend to seek shelter at Le Chambon, a small mountain village in southern France. Pierre Sauvage was born in this peaceful village while his parents were

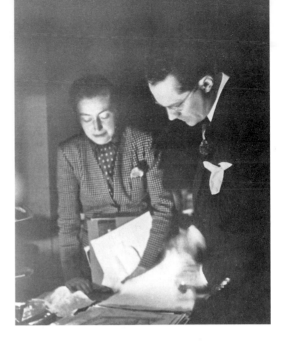

Miriam Davenport with Varian Fry.

in hiding. They and about five thousand other Jews survived the war, sheltered by the Christians who lived in and around Le Chambon. Today Pierre Sauvage is considered an expert on the topic of rescuers of Jews during the Holocaust—the destruction of European Jews by the Nazis during World War II—and is president of the Varian Fry Institute and the Chambon Foundation.

Now that Varian had hired a small staff, they quickly settled into a routine. Varian thought they needed someone who could run errands and asked Miriam if she knew anyone. She did. Miriam had met a seventeen-year-old Jewish boy named Justus Rosenberg when she was in Toulouse. He was currently in Marseilles, and she had helped him find a place to stay. Justus, whom they nicknamed Gussie, looked much younger than he was and appeared angelic with blond hair and blue eyes. Gussie had grown up in the Free City of Danzig (today known as Gdansk), located in northern Poland. Gussie's parents, sensing that Hitler could be dangerous, thought their son would be safer if he went to school in Paris. Then, when Paris was conquered by Hitler, Gussie moved south with all the other refugees. He didn't know what had happened to his parents, and they didn't know what had happened to him. Gussie became the youngest member of Varian's team, acting as its courier: taking messages, documents, papers, money, and parcels to refugees in hiding.

Gussie on La Canebière, the main street in Marseilles.

Although they were help-ing Varian with the refugees, Beamish, Franzi, Lena, and Gussie were refugees them-selves. It was understood that when the opportunity came, each of the office staff members would flee France for his or her own protection.

Varian and his staff began each day at eight in the morn-ing, when the first refugee in line was allowed into the hotel room. Each refugee was interviewed by one of the team, and any relevant information was written down on file cards. For desks, the team used the one small table in the room and a mirror that they took from the back of the dresser. Varian pre-ferred to stand up or sit on the edge of the bed. The afternoon sun shone in the windows of the hotel room, making it feel like an oven. When the heat became unbearable, Varian took off his jacket and tie and rolled up his sleeves.

Some refugees on the lists drawn up by the Emergency Rescue Committee had been wealthy writers, artists, and scientists. But when they had to run for their lives, they left their earthly possessions in homes to which they could never return. Even though some of them had money deposited in banks around the world, they had no access to their accounts because the Nazis controlled all communication coming in and out of their territories. After living lives of wealth and privilege, being destitute was more than some could handle, and they had nervous breakdowns.

Since many refugees needed to be under a doctor's care not only for emotional troubles, but also for physical ones, Varian brought in Marcel Verzeano to help them. Verzeano was a Romanian who had just graduated from medical school in Paris. He spoke several languages fluently. He joined Varian's staff as a doctor, but soon he began working on the undercover side as well. To conceal the handsome, dark-haired young doctor's identity, he was known only as Maurice.

Regardless of whether they had been rich or poor, the refugees were treated with dignity on entering Varian's door. For the documentary *And Crown Thy Good: Varian Fry in Marseille*, Miriam Davenport said, "Although I am terrible at faces and names, to this day, at that time I never forgot a name. Because that was all that these poor souls had—were their names."

All the refugees had something else in common: fear. Each of them knew the Vichy police could come at any moment. If arrested, they would be sent to a concentration camp or handed over to the Gestapo. Some had already been imprisoned in concentration camps from which they had either escaped or been released. By the time they met with Varian's team, they were exhausted, terrified, and nervous. Most had dodged the machine-gun bullets that rained down from Nazi airplanes as they escaped Paris. With little to eat, they had walked hundreds of miles through the French countryside toward Marseilles. They slept in open fields or barns along the way, and every unexpected sound and movement filled them with terror.

Often refugees who had waited patiently in the lobby became

hysterical from fear, stress, and desperation when it was their turn to speak to Varian. Lena, Varian's secretary, had an incredible ability to calm them down. She would step in and say, "You must not go too far." Varian could never understand why it worked, but Lena's words always snapped them out of their panic.

Except for those who were on Varian's official lists, everyone else who came to his door was a stranger to him. They could be telling him the truth or they could be spies sent by the police or Gestapo to find out what he was doing. Varian made a rule his team would never break, that they would help to escape from France only refugees known by people they trusted.

By the end of Varian's second week in Marseilles, the line of people outside his door was so long that the hotel management complained. Varian told the refugees they would have to wait in the lobby and be called up by telephone one at a time.

At the end of every day, when the last refugee left, the most difficult work of all was still ahead for Varian and his team. Of the many refugees they had interviewed throughout the day, the team then had to choose which ones they would try to help. The decisions were made in the bathroom. Varian understood that his hotel room might be bugged. It was also possible that police officials were in the next room, listening through the locked connecting door. So to be safe, the team ran water in the sink and bathtub. They could hear each other as they discussed the refugees, but if the police were listening, the water would make it impossible for them to understand.

Crammed together in the tiny bathroom, the members of the team referred to the file cards filled with information while they discussed the refugees. For Pierre Sauvage's documentary *And Crown Thy Good: Varian Fry in Marseille*, Miriam Davenport described this process:

In the beginning, I was an amateur at this and I thought the others were experienced. So I kept quiet, because I didn't know and I thought the others knew. So I would mention these names and say what they had done, but I just didn't do anything more than that. Whereas they were very upfront about how important these people were. And it was Beamish [Albert Hirschman] who took me aside and said, "Look, these people don't know any more about it than you do. And your clients are going to be sent to the cops and go away and die if you don't defend them. It's up to you to defend them."

He stiffened my backbone, and after that I became as pushy as the others and my clients began to enjoy success.

✳✳✳

Varian and his team wanted to help all of the refugees, but that was impossible. They understood that everything was limited, including money, documents, escape routes, and Varian's time in Marseilles. The reality was that they could help only some of the refugees, and they had to decide which ones. To narrow their choices, they considered whether or not the refugee was in real danger of being arrested because of actions taken against Hitler and the Nazis. They also considered the refugee's contribution to society in the form of politics, art, writing, music, or science.

For Varian, making these "impossible decisions" was the hardest part of his job. He understood what he'd been sent to do. As a representative of the Emergency Rescue Committee, his first obligation was to rescue the refugees on his lists. But after meeting with many refugees, he'd come to believe that some of those on his original lists shouldn't be there. And others who should have been on the lists were not. Most refugees who came to Varian were not successful in the eyes of the world. They were not famous. They were not rich.

But they were mothers, fathers, sons, and daughters. They were valuable. They were in danger. How could he sit in judgment? How could he choose to help Hans Sahl and not to help Léo Sauvage?

Varian wrote:

> We had no way of knowing who was really in danger and who wasn't. We had to guess, and the only safe way to guess was to give each refugee the full benefit of the doubt. Otherwise we might refuse help to someone who was really in danger and learn later that he had been dragged away to Dachau or Buchenwald [concentration camps in Germany] because we had turned him down.

Varian seems to have made peace with his decisions because in a letter to his wife, Eileen, he wrote that "the pleasure of being able to help even a few people more than makes up for the pain of having to turn others down."

Varian Fry appeared to be quiet, serious, and businesslike. But there was another side to his personality that came out with those who got to know him. Even though Varian and his team were discussing life and death, they had fun together. In her memoir, Miriam Davenport wrote:

> With us and with our clients he was warm, sensitive, witty, and relaxed . . . At our conferences in his hotel room . . . he became sometimes playful, sometimes ribald, sometimes raucous. (We all did.) Although we were acutely aware of the gravity of our deliberations and the inevitably tragic consequences of our decisions for many of the supplicants, the atmosphere was far from

conspiratorial or dreary. Occasionally the occupants of neighboring rooms would complain about our loud "parties."

It was near midnight each night before Varian and his team finished deciding which refugees to help. It was better to help some than to help none. From that point on, the refugees they chose would be considered by Varian to be his "protégés" ("protected," in French).

After the choices had been made, Varian had one more job to do before he could go to bed. The list of names, those refugees who were now his protégés, had to be sent by cable to the Emergency Rescue Committee office in New York. The plan was that the home office would then try to get the State Department to issue them American visas.

Each night, around midnight, Beamish accompanied Varian on this last errand of the day. They had to get the cable stamped by the police before it could be sent. They hoped two men would be safer than one as they walked along the narrow backstreets of the city to the nearest police station. The streetlights were so weak that they barely illuminated the way. The city streets that bustled with people during the daylight were empty and silent at this late hour. Except for their own footsteps, the only sounds the two men heard were made by the rats rustling around in the garbage as the men passed by dark alleys.

At last they reached the station, identified with blue lights on either side of the entrance. They went to the telegraph room, where a policeman looked at the cable, then stamped it. As long as the Germans didn't want to arrest a particular refugee, the French police didn't mind how many refugees were granted U.S. visas. To them, every refugee who went to America was one less refugee in France.

Next Varian and Beamish took the cable to the telegraph office, from which it was sent to America. Most nights Varian returned to his room about one in the morning.

For Varian's protégés who were more likely to be wanted by the Gestapo, another system was needed to get their names to the ERC. Since there was always a chance that Vichy police or the Gestapo might read outgoing mail, Varian's team came up with a brilliant plan. Lena typed the names of these refugees on narrow sheets of paper and glued them end to end to make a long strip of paper. She rolled the list up tight, covered it with rubber, and tied the end with thread. She opened the bottom of a tube of toothpaste and slipped the package inside, then carefully closed the tube again. When the next refugee left France, Varian asked that person to pack the toothpaste in his or her suitcase. If border guards searched through the suitcase, they would find just another tube of toothpaste.

Varian told each refugee that on arriving in Lisbon, he or she was to open the tube and retrieve the secret list of names. Then the refugee was to send the list by regular mail to the ERC in New York. Since Portugal was a neutral country in the war, its mail would not be censored, and the list should arrive safely in New York.

The next morning Varian's work started all over again at eight o'clock. Each day a new crowd of refugees waited in the lobby of the Hôtel Splendide to be called up to Varian's room for an interview. Each day the crowd grew larger.

It didn't take long for the police to get suspicious when they heard there was a crowd gathering to see an American. One day they raided the lobby. A "Black Maria," a police van, stopped in front of the Hôtel Splendide with its bell clanging. All of the refugees waiting to see Varian were arrested and piled into the back of the wagon. They were taken to the police station and questioned about Varian's activities. They were then released.

Varian realized he'd made a mistake by not going to Marseilles's chief of police when he first arrived. He should have explained to the chief that the Emergency Rescue Committee planned to assist refugees just as other aid organizations in Marseilles were doing. He should have asked the chief of police for permission to do his work so that the chief would not be suspicious. Varian needed the police to believe that the Emergency Rescue Committee was only a relief agency with nothing to hide.

Varian decided to make an appointment with the chief to explain everything to him. But the morning before the meeting, the phone rang. He picked up the receiver and heard a loud whisper.

"It's the police, old man," Frank Bohn was saying. "Don't worry. We had to expect this. The Consulate will take care of us if anything serious happens. I'm going down now. You'd better look around your room and destroy your papers before they come for you. I'll see you downstairs."

Varian had no time to lose. He ran to the door and locked it.

His mind raced as he thought about all the papers in his room that could prove he was involved in illegally helping enemies of the Nazis escape.

He emptied his pockets of handwritten lists and notes and pitched them in the middle of the bed. Looking around the room, he gathered up various papers detailing possible hiding places, escape routes, and names and contact information for underground workers, and added them to the pile of papers.

Then he grabbed his briefcase, jerked it open, and threw more paper on the pile as he went through the contents. He searched his dresser drawers, books, boxes, and empty suitcases for anything that could incriminate him. He scooped up the pile of papers and ran into the bathroom. Tearing it all into confetti, he sent his priceless information down the toilet.

The only things Varian didn't destroy were his passport, the letter that identified him as an aid worker for the YMCA, and his original lists of refugees from the ERC. He knew the lists could be used against him if the police found them, but he still needed them.

He had to hide the lists. The only place seemed to be behind the mirror on the closet door, where he had already stashed the map of the border crossing that the Austrians had given him. He took out enough screws to loosen the mirror, then dropped the lists between the door and mirror.

Sweat trickled down Varian's face as he replaced each screw.

The sound of the telephone echoed in the room just as his clammy hands finished the job. It was the clerk telling Varian that the police wanted him downstairs.

Varian adjusted his well-fitted jacket and stood as tall as his five-foot-ten-inch frame would allow. He took a final glance around the room and left to face the police.

The police inspector, dressed in a dark business suit, waited for him. He questioned Varian about what he was doing in Marseilles. Varian showed the policeman his passport and letter from the YMCA, and explained that he was helping refugees obtain visas and giving them money to live on while they waited for their documents to be approved. Varian knew it was legal to help refugees try to get visas to leave France as long as they were not wanted by the Gestapo.

In *Assignment: Rescue*, Varian wrote that after the inspector finished interviewing him, he gave Varian the following sly warning:

"Well, I can see nothing wrong. You have a proper letter from a neutral organization. Everything you are doing seems to be legal."

"Oh, I assure you it is," I said.

"We get many reports at Police Headquarters," he said. "People who are angry because their requests for visas are turned down, people who want to collect a reward for turning in a secret agent or spy, people who will squeal on anyone just to get in good with the police. You understand, we have to check out all these reports, in case some high official of the government in Vichy starts asking questions."

He paused. His voice became very low. "If I had found anything suspicious, it would be necessary for me to arrest you here and now."

He paused again, looking me straight in the eye. "You understand?" he said.

I stared back at him. Then I nodded. "Yes, I understand."

I understood, all right. This man was on my side. He was telling me that as a police inspector he had found nothing wrong with my answers. But, as a Frenchman, he knew I was up to a lot more than I'd told him about. His quiet "You understand?" was a warning. A warning to be much more careful than I had been up to now. Otherwise, I'd land in prison and be expelled from the country, or worse.

He turned to pick up his hat. "Sad days have fallen on France," he said. "It is very bad for the refugees. Especially those wanted by the Gestapo. Soon we will have to pick many of them up. Arrest them. Surrender them to the Nazis."

He turned back to me. "I am glad you are helping them," he said. Then he added quickly, "By giving them money, I mean."

With that subtle warning, the police inspector shook hands with Varian and was gone. And so was all the information Varian had destroyed.

[Plans]

THE NEXT DAY VARIAN ATTENDED HIS MEETING WITH the chief of police at the police department. He explained that he was in Marseilles to give aid to refugees. The policeman looked at him as if he suspected Varian was up to no good and warned him that France would welcome his committee if it did nothing illegal. Varian acted shocked at the idea that he might do anything contrary to the laws of the Vichy government in France.

Varian asked, and received, official permission to set up a relief committee. He named his organization the Centre Américain de Secours—in English, the American Relief Center (ARC).

The number of refugees waiting to see Varian at the newly formed ARC grew daily. Then one day Varian looked around his tiny hotel-room-turned-office and saw Franzi lying in the bathtub, fully dressed, dictating letters to Lena, who was sitting on the floor with her typewriter perched on the bidet. They needed a bigger room.

Varian moved to room 307 in the front of the hotel. He had one of the beds taken out to give his team more working space. The room

Lena Fishman gives money to one of the many refugees the American Relief Center was supporting.

overlooked the busy Boulevard d'Athènes. As the staff worked, they heard the shuffling of people walking to and from the nearby train station. If they looked out the window to the left, they could see over the tops of the plane trees that lined both sides of the street and watch the crowds as they went up and down the beautiful marble staircase that led to the station.

Since the American Relief Center was giving out small amounts of money to meet the daily needs of protégés, Varian realized he needed someone who could keep records of the money. Heinz Ernst Oppenheimer was perfect for the job. Varian called him Oppy. Oppenheimer was a Jew, originally from Germany, who had previously run a relief agency in Holland. He was an expert at keeping books, and kept the ARC's books up to date just in case the police ever looked at them. He also devised ways to hide the money the ARC spent to help refugees leave France.

One night after their usual trip to the police station and post office to send the cable with names, Varian and Beamish retraced their steps back to the hotel. They walked everywhere because there was very little gasoline for automobiles in Marseilles. And what gas there was, was used only by the police. As they made their way through the empty backstreets, they felt the familiar fatigue from the long, busy day.

Suddenly they smelled gasoline fumes, which meant Vichy police must be nearby. The dullness of their exhaustion vanished. Varian and Beamish turned the corner from the side street onto the boulevard where the Hôtel Splendide was located.

They stopped dead in their tracks when they saw it.

A sleek black Mercedes pulled up in front of the hotel. It had a German license plate.

Gestapo!

Varian and Beamish instinctively plastered themselves against the wall of the hotel, in the shadows. The chauffeur opened the rear car door. One after the other, five Gestapo officers climbed out. Each wore shiny black boots, a long gray overcoat, and black gloves, despite the late-summer weather. From where they stood, Varian and Beamish could see the gold-colored eagle and swastika symbol on their caps.

"Heil Hitler," the officers said as they clicked their heels and saluted the chauffeur.

After the chauffeur returned their salute, the officers passed beneath the black wrought-iron overhang at the front entrance to the hotel and disappeared through the revolving door into the lobby.

Varian looked at Beamish, then said, "Well, it looks like the Gestapo has arrived in full force."

Ever since Varian reached Marseilles two weeks before, he'd known Hitler's henchmen were in the city, but to actually see them made him nervous. The Gestapo were always on the prowl, looking for enemies of Hitler and the Nazis, including many of the very refugees Varian was trying to get out of France. If arrested by the Gestapo, the refugees would be imprisoned in a concentration camp or perhaps tortured and killed.

Varian was secretly working against these ruthless men—and the stakes were high. He understood the risks he was taking. This was not a movie or a game. He was involved in a struggle for the lives of thousands of refugees—maybe even for his own. Now that the Gestapo were, apparently, staying at the Hôtel Splendide, it would not be safe for the refugees to come to Varian's room anymore. He would need to find another place to set up the office of the American Relief Center.

A local Jewish merchant who sold small leather goods offered Varian the use of his store rent-free until the end of the year. The man knew what had happened to Jews in other Nazi-controlled cities. When the Germans took over, they forced all businesses operated by Jews to close. The same thing would happen in Marseilles. The merchant decided to close his store on his own terms, instead of being forced out of business by the Nazis.

Varian was grateful for the chance to work from the new office space, on Rue Grignan, while he continued to live at the hotel. He and his team moved into the merchant's old store toward the end of August. While the merchant was taking out his inventory of wallets and handbags, Varian's team was bringing in its files and supplies. Varian bought a symbol of freedom for the office in the form of a large American flag on a six-foot flagpole. Then he opened for business.

Varian was so immersed in the work that August 29, 1940, came and went. It was the day Varian was supposed to fly back to the United States. He was too busy to notice.

At the new location, refugees filled up the waiting room and formed a line that snaked out the door, down the hall, and down the stairs. Varian realized he needed someone who could deal with the crowd and maintain order if necessary. He found the perfect man for the job: an American from Georgia named Charles (Charlie) Fawcett. Twenty-one-year-old Charlie had light, curly hair and spoke with a slow, deep, Southern drawl.

Charlie played the jazz trumpet and was an artist. He'd come to France to support the war effort by working in the American Volunteer Ambulance Corps. After the French army was defeated, the only clothes he had were his uniform. But it made him look "official" as he controlled the crowds.

Charlie also understood the danger Jews faced from the Nazis. At the time, if a Jewish woman was married to an American, she would be released from a concentration camp. So Charlie did what he could and married six different Jewish women in different locations—all at the same time, but on paper only. These women were then released from the camps.

There was one problem with Charlie: He spoke only English, and with a pronounced Southern accent. None of the refugees could understand a single word he said. But it didn't matter. Although the refugees couldn't understand his words, there was something in this Southern gentleman's nature that even the most desperate refugee understood. Everyone loved "Shar-lee."

During Varian's first few weeks in Marseilles, he showed a number of refugees the map the Austrians had left with him, and gave them all the information they needed to climb over the Pyrenees. He explained that they must check in with the Spanish border patrol and get their passports stamped. Varian even sent over the Pyrenees refugees who did not have French exit visas. Among them were Hertha Pauli, the Austrian journalist; Dr. Otto Meyerhof, the German biochemist who won a Nobel Prize in 1922 in the category of Physiology or Medicine; Konrad Heiden, the German author of a biography of Hitler; and Hans Natonek, a Czechoslovakian writer and editor.

Varian Fry at his desk in the office of the American Relief Center.

When his protégés were ready to leave, Varian said goodbye to each of them in exactly the same way. His last words were, "I'll see you soon in New York."

And they believed him.

The French people were split in their loyalties after the German takeover. Some resisted the Nazis and had sympathy for the refugees. Others were willing to go along with whatever the Nazis wanted and didn't care what happened to the refugees.

A refugee encountering a French policeman didn't know where the officer's loyalty lay. Some refugees met sympathetic policemen who even allowed them to take the train across the border without an exit visa. Some met policemen who turned them away at the train station because they didn't have an exit visa. Some refugees who walked over the Pyrenees Mountains encountered kind and helpful border patrols; others did not.

Then, after the refugees made it into Spain, they never knew what would happen. Some Spanish border guards didn't ask and didn't care whether or not a refugee had a French exit visa. Others would not allow a refugee into Spain without a French exit visa and would force the refugee to return to France. And sometimes the Spaniards would refuse to let refugees pass, but would change their minds after accepting a bribe of money or cigarettes.

Every refugee who fled France faced uncertainty and risk.

When Varian arrived each morning, the eyes of all the refugees followed him as he made his way past the line and into the office. He was always dressed in a beautifully tailored suit and tie, complete with handkerchief in the breast pocket. Sometimes he even wore a red carnation in his buttonhole.

The day quickly became a blur of activity. The team compiled list after list of protégés according to their needs, such as one of those who had an American visa but needed a Portuguese visa, and another of those who needed a French safe-conduct visa.

As the boss, Varian met with consuls of various countries, answered countless questions, and solved problems. He also continued meeting with protégés who needed help getting passports, identity papers, military records, visas, and other documents. If possible, he obtained documents in the real names of the protégés. But some of them were well-known enemies of Hitler and wouldn't be safe traveling through France and Spain using their own names. These people needed to have false identities created for them with forged identification cards, passports, and other documents. However, it was Varian's rule that once they arrived in Lisbon and boarded ships bound for the United States, they must use their true identities.

The forged documents had to look genuine. Not only did border guards check the travelers' papers, the police randomly checked the papers of people anywhere, at any time, to see if they were "in order."

Varian found an artist, Wilhelm Spira, who could create perfect forgeries. Originally from Austria, Spira had been a cartoonist in France before the war. He had been imprisoned in a concentration camp and somehow managed to escape. In Marseilles, Spira chose to be known by the name Bill Freier because the German word *freier* means "freer."

Bill Freier (Wilhelm Spira) with Mina.

Bill Freier bought blank identification cards, which were sold in tobacco shops in France, and used them to create identities for Varian's protégés. He had the incredible ability to imitate with a paintbrush the rubber stamp used by the police on official identification cards. To support himself and his fiancée, Mina, Freier charged Varian fifty cents per forged identification card. Varian added Bill Freier and Mina to his list of protégés and sent their names by cable to the New York office in hopes of getting them visas to enter the United States. Unfortunately, a few months later, before he could escape France, Freier was betrayed to the police. When they arrested him, they found his forgery supplies and sent him to Auschwitz, the notorious concentration camp, although first he was allowed to marry Mina.

✳✳✳

Varian Fry actually had two jobs. The first was running the illegal undercover organization that smuggled refugees out of France. The second was running the legal, "cover" operation of a relief committee. This work he wanted the police to know about.

Varian's main objective in Marseilles was to get specific refugees out of France, so the overwhelming majority of people who came to his office did not become his protégés. At the same time, Varian and his team wanted to help every refugee in some way. As part of their cover as a relief committee, they gave refugees meal tickets that had been supplied by the Quakers. They also recommended that the refugees seek additional help at the Committee to Assist Refugees, a Jewish relief organization in Marseilles. This was the only help Varian could give to most of these people.

Varian and his American Relief Center financially supported all the refugees they chose as their protégés. It took a lot of money to pay for their food, shelter, and other necessities until arrangements could be made to get them out of France. Then it took more money to buy train tickets and boat tickets, and to cover other travel expenses when the details of the escapes were finalized. All of the three thousand dollars Varian brought with him to Marseilles—the equivalent of over $44,000 today—was gone by the end of the first two weeks. He had to figure out how to get more money to help the refugees.

Back in the United States, donations to support Varian's work were continually being collected by the Emergency Rescue Committee in New York. The problem for Varian was how to get that money. Because the Vichy government kept track of all money going in and out of France, the usual methods of transferring money were not possible. If Varian repeatedly received large sums of money from America, the police would wonder what he was doing with it. Varian knew he must avoid arousing their suspicions. But somehow he had to get the money.

It didn't take long for Beamish to come up with a plan. When Lena started working for Varian, she took over the interviews that Beamish had been doing. This left street-smart Beamish free to do what he did best: undercover work. Beamish solved all sorts of problems, including where to obtain false passports and identity papers.

And now he'd figured out how to handle the money. He suggested a money exchange—exchanging money from one country for an equal amount from a different country.

Although most refugees were poor, a few of Varian's protégés still had some cash. After Varian made arrangements for their escape, and right before they left France, the refugees gave Varian their French francs (the currency used in 1940). Varian reported that amount to the Emergency Rescue Committee in New York. Then, when the refugees arrived safely in America, instead of going to the bank to exchange their francs for dollars, they went to the ERC office and were given back their money in American dollars. This exchange was advantageous for everyone. Varian got the money the ERC had collected for his work without the police knowing, and the refugees got a good exchange rate. Also, they didn't have to report large sums of money when they passed through border police checkpoints.

The system worked so well that Beamish looked for other people who wanted to exchange French francs for American dollars. The local gangsters in Marseilles knew lots of people who wanted to get their money out of Europe. Beamish arranged for the gangsters to be the middlemen in the money exchange. And of course they took a percentage for their services. This way, the money donated in America was always available to Varian in Marseilles without the police finding out about it.

Another solution to the money problem came in the form of Mary Jayne Gold, a blond, beautiful, wealthy American woman. Before the war, Mary Jayne had traveled all over Europe, from the beaches of the Riviera to the ski slopes in Switzerland. She owned and flew her own airplane from place to place. Mary Jayne hated the Nazis and had contributed to the war effort by donating her Vega Gull airplane to the French army. She was in Paris when the Germans defeated

Mary Jayne Gold.

the French, and joined the exodus of millions as they fled south. And like most of them, she ended up in Marseilles.

According to her memoir *Crossroads Marseilles 1940*, Mary Jayne Gold ran into Miriam Davenport in Marseilles. They had known each other previously and resumed their friendship. One day at the Pelikan café, one of their favorite hangouts, they were discussing the refugee situation. Miriam told Mary Jayne that the money at the ARC was running low. Mary Jayne said she could give them some money. She also suggested that if Varian could help her exchange her American money, she would give them even more. Mary Jayne wanted to work against the Nazis and help refugees in any way she could, so she suggested to Miriam that she "might even do some interviewing for them or something."

Miriam had already told Varian about Mary Jayne. She'd said that Mary Jayne would probably be willing to donate money to their work. But Varian was wary of her. In her book, Mary Jayne explained that Varian thought her high-society life "sounded frivolous and he assured Miriam that I must be exactly the kind of American who surrounded herself with the most reactionary Europeans with fancy titles. I was not to be trusted."

It was only after Varian met Mary Jayne that he agreed to let her work with the team. Mary Jayne started out interviewing refugees. True to her word, she continually contributed money to the ARC.

Mary Jayne understood that Varian's mission was to rescue well-known writers, artists, and scientists. But she wondered who would help the many refugees who were not famous. She decided that her donations must be used to help refugees who were not on the ERC list. Miriam called refugees who benefited from Mary Jayne's money the "Gold List." One of the men who escaped France because of the Gold List was Karel (Charles) Sternberg, a refugee from Czechoslovakia who would later become the director of the International Rescue Committee.

✳✳✳

Around the beginning of September, Varian received a postcard from a prison in Figueras, Spain. Five of his protégés had crossed the border into Spain and had been arrested and thrown into prison. Varian didn't know what had gone wrong. He wondered if they hadn't checked in at the border as he'd told them to do.

To prevent this from happening again, Varian considered having a guide lead refugees over the mountain to show them the way and point out to them where to check in at the border. It would be safer for the refugees, but dangerous for the guide, Varian, and everyone who worked at the American Relief Center. Helping refugees escape France was a violation of Article 19 in the armistice agreement. If anyone connected with the ARC was arrested for leading refugees out of France, the Gestapo would find out what Varian was doing. If caught red-handed, the team could no longer claim they were just another aid organization.

Varian had to decide whether to protect his protégés as they crossed the border, or protect himself and the rest of the team. He chose to protect the refugees.

The first person who guided Varian's protégés over the mountain pass was Leon (Dick) Ball, an American from Montana. Ball was a friend of Charlie Fawcett's from the ambulance corps. He owned a lard factory in France and traveled all over the country selling his product, so he knew his way around. Before working with Varian, Ball had been helping refugees in any way he could. He also helped English soldiers get out of France. But he had a tendency to brag about what he'd done. Ball peppered everything he said with vulgar expressions, whether he was speaking French or English. Just to hear him talk, one might think he was a thug, but Varian described Ball as a "rough diamond, a knight in overalls." Every other day or so, beginning in early September, Ball led a group of two or three refugees at a time over the Pyrenees. With each trip he made, this rough-talking lard salesman risked his own freedom to guide complete strangers safely across the border into Spain.

[Escape]

NOW VARIAN KNEW THE WHEREABOUTS OF THREE OF HIS
most famous protégés: Lion Feuchtwanger, Franz Werfel, and Heinrich Mann. The Feuchtwangers were hiding at Bingham's villa. Franz
and Alma Werfel, whom Varian had met on his first night in Marseilles, were staying in a local hotel. Heinrich Mann and his wife,
Nelly, had recently arrived in the city and were also at a local hotel.
None of them had a French exit visa or transit visa, and these documents would never be granted to them in Vichy France because each
had expressed anti-Nazi sentiments. All were wanted by the Gestapo.

Bohn had been working on arrangements to have a boat in the
harbor take out a load of refugees. At first Varian thought this would
be the best way to get his famous clients out of the country. But the
police were closely watching the port of Marseilles. When Varian's
team had supplies loaded onto a boat in the harbor, the police became
suspicious and placed a guard on the boat. After all the time and
money Bohn had invested in making arrangements for the boat, the
plan had to be abandoned.

Varian went to Harry Bingham's villa to tell Lion Feuchtwanger that their plan to get him out by boat was impossible. Without an exit visa allowing him to leave France legally, probably his only choice was to cross on foot over the Pyrenees Mountains into Spain, and from there, take a train to Lisbon, like many others before him. Varian asked Feuchtwanger if he would be willing to try this.

"If you will come with me, of course I will," Feuchtwanger answered.

Varian agreed. Then he decided that since he would accompany Lion and Marta Feuchtwanger to Lisbon, he might as well take Franz and Alma Werfel, and Heinrich and Nelly Mann, too.

Besides wanting to make sure his famous protégés got out of France, Varian had other reasons to go to Lisbon. First, he needed to write a letter to the leaders of the Emergency Rescue Committee. Varian knew the Vichy police might be reading all of his outgoing mail, and he needed to honestly explain in a letter the situation in Marseilles. Because Portugal was a neutral country, he could safely mail such a letter from Lisbon.

Varian had already stayed longer than planned. The leaders of the ERC were pressuring him to come back to the United States. Varian planned to write them that his mission, arranging for prominent refugees to escape Europe, was more complicated than they had realized. The job could not be completed in a couple of weeks. Now that he was in Marseilles, Varian understood that the work must be ongoing. As long as the Nazis were in control of Europe, refugees would be in danger. Varian would ask the ERC to send someone to replace him. He was willing to go back home, but he felt he couldn't leave until someone took his place. In the three weeks that he'd been in Marseilles, Varian had hired a team of people to help him, worked out endless details for escapes, and succeeded in getting refugees out of Europe. He couldn't leave Marseilles without explaining the work to his replacement.

The second reason Varian needed to make the trip was to check on the five refugees who had been arrested as they traveled through Spain. Varian wanted to find out why they had been imprisoned and see if he could help them. Conditions in Spain had not been good since the Spanish Civil War had ended the year before, in 1939. The war had lasted nearly three years before Francisco Franco became victorious. Spain was left in ruins and many of its people were destitute and hungry. When Franco took over, he installed a Fascist form of government, in which one central leader, a dictator, suppresses any opposition by force.

Although Spain was considered neutral in the war that now gripped most of Europe, Franco was more sympathetic toward Germany because its leader, Hitler, was also a Fascist dictator.

The third and final reason for going was that Varian and all of his team wanted some soap. Because of the shortages of supplies during the war, soap was impossible to get in either France or Spain. Varian planned to buy it in Lisbon—lots of it.

Varian understood how risky it would be to take Feuchtwanger, Werfel, Mann, and their wives to Lisbon. If they were caught traveling through the countryside without French transit visas, they could be arrested. And if they were caught trying to cross the French border without French exit visas, they could be arrested. It would be a gamble every step of the way. Vichy policemen were everywhere, and a refugee never knew what would happen when stopped by one of them. Some policemen helped the refugees; others were glad to arrest them.

Normally a traveler arriving in the small French border town of

Cerbère boarded a train that crossed the international border into Spain. But these weren't normal times. Now if a refugee could not take the train at Cerbère, the only option for leaving France was to walk over the Pyrenees Mountains that loomed just behind Cerbère.

From the reports of protégés who had made it to Lisbon, Varian learned that the experience varied. Some said the border police allowed them on the train without exit visas. Others said the police intentionally looked the other way, pretending not to notice as they boarded the train. And others reported that the police refused to allow them on the train without exit visas, and that they crossed over the mountains. So far none had been arrested at the border, not even those without exit visas. But the border situation was constantly changing, and no one knew when the border might close permanently. Understanding all the dangers, Varian believed the Feuchtwangers, Manns, and Werfels should try to leave.

The Werfels had Czech passports in their own names. Although the Manns were Germans, a few years before, they had been made honorary Czech citizens and given Czech passports. Only the Feuchtwangers did not have valid passports. They were from Germany and therefore were officially stateless. However, the Feuchtwangers did have an "affidavit in lieu of passport" issued to them by the United States, which could serve as a passport for stateless refugees such as themselves. Marta Feuchtwanger's affidavit was issued in her own name because she was not wanted by the Gestapo. Lion's affidavit was issued in the false name James Wetcheek. This was a pen name he'd used before, a sort of play on the name Feuchtwanger. In German, *feucht* means "wet" and *Wange* means "cheek"—Wetcheek.

As the final preparations for the trip were made, Varian heard a rumor that Spain would not allow any stateless refugees into the country. With all sorts of rumors circulating at all times, Varian wasn't sure whether this one was true or not. But he decided it was too risky for Marta and Lion Feuchtwanger to make the trip if there was a chance that they would be turned away at the Spanish border. He assured them that if he got to the border and found the rumor false, he would let them know by cable.

Although now the Feuchtwangers would not be going, Varian continued with his plans to accompany the Werfels and the Manns. Heinrich Mann asked if his nephew Golo Mann could go with them, and Varian agreed. Golo was the son of the Nobel Prize–winning author Thomas Mann, who was giving lectures at Princeton University in New Jersey.

Not long before Varian left for Lisbon with his protégés, he was approached by an Italian political refugee named Emilio Lussu. He suggested that Varian contact the British and arrange with them to have boats come to a port off the coast of France to rescue Italian and Spanish refugees. Lussu himself was an expert in the art of escape and gave Varian detailed nautical maps of the French Mediterranean coast indicating places where explosive mines had been spread by the Nazis. Lussu also provided Varian with a complex code system he could use to communicate with the British.

Before sunrise on September 12, Varian left his hotel and walked under the plane trees that lined the sidewalk of the Boulevard d'Athènes. It was only one block to the massive staircase that led up to the Gare Saint-Charles. Varian was the first of the group to arrive. He was ready to accompany Franz and Alma Werfel, Heinrich and Nelly Mann, and Golo Mann in their escape from France. Dick Ball was going along to guide them over the Pyrenees Mountains if necessary.

Varian stood in the station clutching his suitcase nervously. The reality of what he was doing settled in on him. Hidden underneath the lining of the case were the nautical charts of minefields that Lussu had given him. Also in his possession was information written in code. If the police searched and found these, he would surely be arrested. It didn't calm Varian's nerves to see Franz and Alma Werfel arrive with twelve suitcases, one filled with the scores of Gustav Mahler's symphonies. Apparently, it never occurred to Alma to leave anything behind as they were running for their lives.

The train trip from Marseilles to Cerbère took all day. They pulled into the station after dark, and the seven of them got off the train. When Varian saw that each passenger was being asked to show travel papers, he felt a sense of panic. He was the only one who had both a French safe-conduct pass and an exit visa. None of his group had the right papers to even travel to the border of France, much less cross it. Clearly there was no way to avoid having their papers checked. Ball stepped up and gathered all of their passports and went into the police office. Like Varian, he knew that some refugees who'd passed through Cerbère had been allowed to cross the border into Spain by train even without a French exit visa. Ball hoped the policeman he encountered would be one who was sympathetic toward refugees.

Ball tried to get the policeman to let them take the train. The man agreed to think it over until the next morning. The travelers stayed overnight in a local hotel to await his answer.

In the morning Dick Ball went back to the policeman. Rejoining the group, he told them the bad news: the policeman could not allow them on the train because his supervisor was there. He recommended to Ball that the group get out of France while they could by walking over the Pyrenees. Then the policeman had pointed out to Ball the best path to take up the mountain.

Varian looked at the mountains that loomed above the town. What should they do now? Then he looked at Franz Werfel, who was fifty years old and overweight and had a heart condition. Heinrich Mann was almost seventy. Could Franz and Heinrich make it over the rough terrain on foot? He suspected the other three would be fine: Alma Werfel was sixty-one but seemed to be strong enough, Nelly Mann was forty-two years old, and Golo Mann was thirty-one.

The temperature was already rising, promising a hot September day. Varian wondered if he should try to buy forged exit visas and hope they could get through later on a train. Might the Spanish border close permanently before he could arrange for the false visas?

The little group gathered together. They must decide what to do. Silently each looked into the faces of the others. All considered the options. Should they walk over the mountains to cross the border into Spain? Or should they go back to Marseilles and hope to make other arrangements at a later time?

In *Surrender on Demand* Varian wrote about what happened after they asked him for advice:

"Well," I said, measuring my words very carefully, "if you think you can make it, I'd advise you to go over the hill today. We know it can be done today. We don't know what will happen tomorrow or the day after."

Heinrich Mann, Golo Mann and Mrs. Werfel decided immediately to go. But Werfel and Mrs. Mann were hesitant. Werfel looked at the hill and sighed. Suddenly he remembered it was Friday the 13th, and he began to quaver.

"It's an unlucky day," he said. "Don't you think we'd better wait until tomorrow?"

But Mrs. Werfel quickly put a stop to that line.

"*Das ist Unsinn* [That is nonsense], *Franz*," she said, with emphasis, and Werfel lapsed into silence. But whenever he looked at the hill, he gave a deep sigh.

Mrs. Mann began talking hurriedly to her husband in German.

"Listen, Heinrich," she said, "Mr. Fry is a very nice young man. He says he comes to save us. But how do we know? Maybe he is a spy come to lead us into a trap. I think we ought not to do what he advises."

"*Verzeihung, Frau Mann,*" I said, in my best German, "*aber vielleicht wissen Sie nicht dass ich Deutsch verstehe.*" [Excuse me, Mrs. Mann, perhaps you do not know that I understand German.]

Mrs. Mann blushed crimson at this, and we heard no more from her.

Finally all of them agreed to go over the Pyrenees without delay. Now that the decision had been made, Varian took over once again. Since his papers were in order and he could cross the border safely, he would take all the luggage on the train with him—all seventeen pieces. The others would cross the mountains on foot. They would meet at the end of the day at the train station in Portbou, Spain.

The Werfels would travel under their real names with their Czech passports. Golo Mann would use his American affidavit in his real name. The Manns had a choice to make. They had genuine Czech passports in their real names, and they also had American papers using the names Mr. and Mrs. Heinrich Ludwig. They decided they might be safer traveling through the Spanish border using the American documents.

After the Manns decided to travel as the Ludwigs, Varian asked both of them to go through their suitcases, pockets, and Mrs. Mann's handbag and give him everything that had the Mann name on it, such as cards and letters. Varian wanted to be sure there was nothing in their possession that would cause them a problem.

Varian looked at Heinrich Mann, a dignified, well-dressed elderly gentleman who had fled Germany when the Nazis came to power. Varian asked Mann to take off his hat. Heinrich Mann handed it to Varian without a word.

Varian took out his penknife and scratched out the initials on the hatband. When Varian looked up, he saw sadness on Mann's face.

"We are obliged to act like real criminals!" said Heinrich Mann.

There was no time to lose. Varian gave the refugees cigarettes to use as "gifts" for the border patrol officers. He watched them as they started up the hill and disappeared from sight. He hoped he would see them later that day at the train station in Portbou.

Varian waited at the station for the train to leave that afternoon. He worried about what the police inspectors would think when they saw he had seventeen pieces of luggage, some filled with women's clothes. But when an officer searched the luggage, he didn't seem to care how many suitcases Varian had, or what was in them.

After he was safely on the train, Varian decided to get rid of all the papers he'd collected from Mr. and Mrs. Mann. He went into the restroom and set them on fire. As smoke filled the tiny compartment, he was afraid to open the door in case someone noticed and began asking questions. It wasn't long before the smoke was so heavy that he had to crouch down on the floor to breathe. As soon as all that was left of the Manns' papers was ash, Varian flushed it down the toilet.

When Varian arrived in the Spanish border town of Portbou, the Spanish customs officer searched his seventeen bags with the same boredom that the Frenchman had. Varian made his way to a local hotel, paying a porter to help him with all the baggage. When he returned to the station, he expected to find the Werfels and Manns waiting.

They were not there.

Where could they be? All sorts of horrible scenarios flashed through Varian's mind as he looked around the train station. He paced up and down the platform.

Finally he hired a young man to go to the police station to see if his "friends" had been arrested. They hadn't. The young man suggested that Varian go up to the guard shack on the highway and inquire there.

Varian followed the road up the hot, dusty hill to the guard shack. Beside it a black-and-white-striped barrier stretched across the road, indicating the border between Spain and France. Varian approached the guards and gave them cigarettes. He asked if they had seen five travelers and described them.

The guards led Varian into the guard shack and told him to wait.

As Varian sat there, he wondered where his protégés were. He also wondered if he was going to be arrested. He smoked one cigarette after another.

At last, one of the guards came back in and told him that his friends were at the train station. Relief washed over Varian. He gave the guard all the rest of his cigarettes, shook his hand, and ran out the door. Varian hurried down the hill, nearly running toward the station. He saw his five protégés. They ran into each other's arms with joy and relief.

The climb had been difficult, especially for seventy-year-old Heinrich Mann. The path was so steep that Dick Ball and Golo Mann had to almost carry him most of the way. Alma Mahler Werfel would later write in her book *And the Bridge Is Love* that they started up the hill and the "steep stony trail that soon vanished altogether. It was sheer slippery terrain that we crawled up, bounded by precipices. Mountain goats could hardly have kept their footing on the glassy, shimmering slate. If you skidded, there was nothing but thistles to hold on to."

At the top of the hill, out of nowhere, two French border guards came toward them. Each refugee expected to be arrested and sent to a concentration camp. And there was no sense in running, for the guards would simply shoot them. They just stood there, awaiting arrest.

Varian describes the scene in *Surrender on Demand*:

When the *gardes mobiles* reached them, they saluted.

"Are you looking for Spain?" one of them asked.

Somebody said yes.

"Well," the guard said, "follow the footpath here to the left. If you take the one to the right, it will lead you to the French border post, and if you haven't got exit visas you may get into trouble. But if you follow the left-hand path it will take you straight to the Spanish border point, and if you report there and don't try to go around it, you'll be all right."

They immediately headed down the hill single file toward the Spanish border point. When they arrived, the Werfels and Manns had no trouble. But one of the guards was more interested in Golo Mann. His papers said he was going to America to visit his father, Thomas Mann, who had been awarded the Nobel Prize in Literature in 1929. Thomas Mann had left Germany when Hitler came to power, and later had his citizenship taken away.

In *Surrender on Demand*, Varian described what happened after the guard considered Golo's papers:

"So you are the son of Thomas Mann?" the sentry asked.

Through Golo's mind flashed visions of Gestapo lists. He felt his doom was imminent, but he decided to play out his role heroically to the end.

"Yes," he said. "Does that displease you?"

"On the contrary," the sentry answered. "I am honored to make the acquaintance of the son of so great a man." And he shook hands with Golo. Then he telephoned down to the station and had a car come up to get them.

[Spy]

WHEN THE EXCITEMENT OF THE REUNION HAD PASSED, Varian asked the customs officers if they were allowing into Spain people whose citizenship had been stripped by the Nazis. The officer told him that these people could travel through Spain. The rumor Varian had heard in Marseilles was false. Lion Feuchtwanger and his wife could have entered Spain with the others, after all. As promised, Varian cabled a message to Lena in Marseilles telling her that "it would be all right for Harry to send his friends, after all."

Varian had been in Europe long enough to understand that France, Spain, and Portugal constantly changed the "rules" of border crossings. And this trip had proved once again that the refugees never knew if they would encounter an official who would help them in some way, or arrest them.

Varian's group took a train through Barcelona and on to Madrid. In Madrid, he arranged for airplane tickets to Lisbon, from which the Werfels and all three of the Manns would eventually board a ship to the United States.

This photo appeared in the newspaper after the Manns and the Werfels arrived in the United States. From left to right: Thomas Mann (Heinrich's brother), who had come to meet them, Nelly Mann, Heinrich Mann, Franz Werfel, and Dr. Frank Kingdon, the president of the Emergency Rescue Committee, who welcomed them.

While in Madrid, Varian took the nautical charts out of his suitcase lining and went to the British Embassy. He wanted to discuss with the British the possibility of their sending boats to the port of Marseilles to get refugees out of France. Varian still hoped that some of his protégés could be taken out by boat. But he was also concerned about the well-known political refugees—the people in Frank Bohn's care—who had fled Spain and Italy.

Like Spain, Italy was a Fascist country, under the control of the dictator Benito Mussolini. Anyone who had opposed Francisco Franco in Spain or Mussolini in Italy had fled to safety in Marseilles—just as the Jews and anti-Nazis had fled there from Germany's dictator, Hitler.

While some of Varian's refugees were successfully climbing over the Pyrenees and traveling through Spain to Lisbon, that method of escape was impossible for a man like Francisco Largo Caballero. He had been the Prime Minister in Spain, and Franco wanted him dead. Since most people in Spain would recognize him, he could not travel through the country without being arrested. Also, there were men from Italy who could not safely travel through Spain without being recognized. One was Giuseppe Modigliani, who had been the Socialist Party leader in Italy. For men such as Caballero and Modigliani, the best chance of escape was to leave Marseilles by boat.

When Varian arrived at the British Embassy in Madrid, he met with Major Torr, the British military attaché officer. Varian said he hoped the British could send a ship to Marseilles to get refugees out by sea. But Varian found out that the British had the same problem. Many British soldiers were trapped in France and were considered enemies. Although the Royal Navy wanted to get these soldiers out, it would not allow one of its ships to separate from the rest of the fleet to go get them.

Still, Major Torr was determined to find a way to get the soldiers out of France and to British territory at the Rock of Gibraltar. Gibraltar, only three miles long and one half mile wide, was a British territory located on the southern tip of Spain at the entrance to the Mediterranean Sea. But there was no clear solution to the problem of how to get refugees and soldiers out of Marseilles by sea. Since Varian was on his way to Lisbon, Major Torr asked him to come back to discuss the issue further when he returned to Madrid on his way to Marseilles.

After his meeting at the British Embassy, Varian traveled on to Lisbon. From there he wrote a letter, as he'd planned, explaining the situation in Marseilles to the Emergency Rescue Committee. And he could not forget his other purpose in Lisbon. Lena had filled his baggage with little notes reminding Varian of one thing. In every language she knew, Lena had written the word "soap." A note written in Polish drifted to the floor when Varian pulled out a clean shirt. When he put on a pair of socks, he found a note in Russian crammed into the toe. Knowing he could not return empty-handed, Varian bought about three dozen cakes of soap.

While in Lisbon, Varian met with Dr. Charles Joy, the leader of the Unitarian Service Committee, who had set up an office there to help refugees. At Dr. Joy's office, he was happy to see the familiar face of Franzi, who had recently arrived in Lisbon with his family. He was doing everything he could to help Dr. Joy while waiting to leave for America. Franzi was the first of Varian's staff to leave; many of the others would eventually do the same. Varian also met with some of the refugees who had safely made it to Lisbon with his help, including the Manns.

On the return trip to Marseilles, Varian stopped at the British Embassy in Madrid as planned. He hoped that he could help figure out a way to get people out of Marseilles by sea. This time he met with Sir Samuel Hoare, the British ambassador in Spain.

Sir Samuel asked Varian if he could get British soldiers across the border. The Spanish government had agreed to allow British soldiers to travel through Spain as they went south to rejoin their countrymen at Gibraltar. So the British knew that if they could get their soldiers from France across the border into Spain, they would be safe.

"I am willing to place $10,000 at your disposal. Are you willing to undertake to send our men across the frontier into Spain and at the same time try to organize escapes by boat? If you succeed in finding boats, you can send your refugees and our men on them," said Sir Samuel.

Varian was surprised. Basically, the ambassador was asking Varian to help British soldiers across the Spanish border in the same way he'd been helping his own protégés to cross it, rather than sending boats for them.

This could be dangerous for Varian. He needed to consider the offer carefully. Because Britain and Germany were at war, if Varian was caught helping the British military, the Nazis would consider him an enemy spy—and he would be treated accordingly, regardless of the fact that he was an American. Varian understood that his mission in Europe on behalf of the Emergency Rescue Committee was to arrange the escape of specific intellectual refugees—not trapped British soldiers. And yet Varian hoped that if he helped the British, he could eventually find a boat that could take both his protégés and the soldiers out of France.

With a handshake, Varian accepted the deal.

At Varian's suggestion, Sir Samuel consented to exchange the ten thousand dollars through the ERC office in New York. He also agreed that from that moment on, any communication between the embassy and Varian would be made through the secret code Lussu had worked out.

Continuing from Madrid toward Marseilles, Varian stopped next in Barcelona. There he found out why the five refugees had been arrested. As he suspected, they had not checked in with the border guards as they'd been told to do. Later, when they were caught in Spain without entrance stamps on their papers, they were arrested and charged with clandestine entry and smuggling. Varian hired a local lawyer who worked to get them out of jail.

When Varian reached Marseilles, during the third week of September, the strong, cold wind from the north, called the mistral, whipped through the city. Low, gray clouds hung overhead as Varian descended the huge staircase outside the train station and met up with Beamish and Lena. In the ten days or so that Varian had been away, things had changed in the city. Supplies of all kinds were running low. At their breakfast together, the coffee wasn't really coffee but mostly burnt grain. Saccharin had replaced sugar. The bread was stale. And there was no butter.

When Varian handed Lena four bars of soap, she was delighted. The rest he divided among all the others in the office.

Beamish and Lena brought him up to date on all that had been happening. After getting Varian's message that it was safe, the Feuchtwangers left France. They were assisted on the way to America by Martha and Waitstill Sharp, who worked with the Unitarian Service Committee on behalf of refugees.

Also, during Varian's absence, the police had complained to the American Embassy about Varian, saying they were uneasy about the "activities of Dr. Bohn and Mr. Fry." Varian was not sure what the police or the embassy would do next. He was not ready to leave Marseilles; there were too many refugees who needed to get out. Varian decided to visit Hugh Fullerton, consul general at the American Consulate in Marseilles.

Fullerton told Varian to leave France as soon as possible, before he was forced out or arrested. When Varian asked what the police had said about him, the consul general refused to tell him. He also refused to tell Varian what he had written to the State Department in Washington in response.

However, Fullerton did show Varian the reply he got back from the State Department. It said:

THIS GOVERNMENT CANNOT COUNTENANCE THE ACTIVITIES
AS REPORTED OF DR. BOHN AND MR. FRY AND OTHER
PERSONS IN THEIR EFFORTS IN EVADING THE LAWS OF
COUNTRIES WITH WHICH THE UNITED STATES MAINTAINS
FRIENDLY RELATIONS.

To come to Marseilles, Varian had been issued an American passport that was valid for six months, from June 22, 1940, to January 22,

1941. But after seeing this response from the State Department, Varian realized that the American Embassy, which was located in Vichy, might recall his passport. So he contacted the embassy to ask it to refrain from doing so until he could appear in person to explain the legal relief work he was doing. The embassy told him not to bother to travel to Vichy. It had already sent its report about Varian to the State Department.

The American Embassy in Vichy, the American Consulate in Marseilles, and the U.S. State Department all wanted Varian to leave—but this resistance made him even more determined not to go, at least not voluntarily. He knew, however, that the Vichy police could arrest him and force him out of France at any time.

Varian was also being pressured to leave by the ERC and by his wife. Eileen had expected him back at the end of August and wanted to know when he was coming home. Varian sent her a cable on September 25, 1940. To save money, his message was short and combined words.

RETURNING SOONAS SUCCESSOR ARRIVES **stop** WELL LOVE FRY

Varian hoped his wife would understand that he needed to stay on and that she would convince the ERC of it. He sent her another cable on October 1, 1940:

OFFICE HERE WOULD COLLAPSE IF I LEFT NOW PERSUADE
THEM SEND SUCCESSOR IMMEDIATELY LETME STAY UNTIL HE
ARRIVES **stop** . . . HUNDREDS HAVE COME DEPEND ONME
FOR MONEY ADVICE COMFORT **stop** LEAVING NOW WOULD BE
CRIMINALLY IRRESPONSIBLE **stop** COUNTING ONYOU EXPLAIN
ARRANGE **stop** MUCH LOVE FRY

Similar pressure was put on Frank Bohn. While Varian decided to stay, Bohn chose to return to America. But before Bohn's departure in early October, he asked Varian to take over the refugees he'd been trying to help, such as Rudolf Hilferding, who had previously been a German Minister of Finance, and Rudolf Breitscheid, who had once been the leader in Germany of the Social Democratic Party. How could Varian refuse to do what he could for them?

Now Varian felt he was responsible for finding a way out of France for all of his own protégés, the trapped British soldiers, and Bohn's political and labor leaders. Their lives were in his hands.

The pressure on Varian to go back to America increased from every direction. The American government wanted to stay out of the war and didn't want an American citizen causing problems in Europe. Almost every day the American Consulate in Marseilles contacted Varian to ask him when he was leaving. The State Department in Washington, D.C., pushed the Emergency Rescue Committee in New York to recall Varian. The ERC insisted that Varian come back to the United States.

And Eileen wrote Varian on October 19, 1940:

I hope you realize that the reason I stopped writing to you over a month ago was because I supposed that you would be back here "next week" from Sept. 20 on . . . I sometimes wonder whether you will ever come back, and if you do whether you'll be able to stand the monotony.

Despite all the pressure to go back home, Varian stayed to help his protégés escape. But he had another, more personal, reason: someone had challenged his abilities.

He'd heard this in a roundabout way. Charlie Fawcett had a

friend whose cousin was in the German army. Through this connection, Charlie found out that the Germans knew about Varian and his work. A German officer visiting Charlie's friend in Marseilles said, "Sure, we know all about Fry. We know he's trying to get our political enemies out of France. We aren't worrying. We're confident he won't succeed."

Varian was determined to prove them wrong. Although it was impossible to keep exact records, by this time Varian had probably helped two hundred or more refugees out of France, including Franz Werfel, Heinrich Mann, Lion Feuchtwanger, Hertha Pauli, Konrad Heiden, Otto Meyerhof, and their families. Varian intended to do everything in his power to rescue many more. And it didn't matter how much pressure the U.S. State Department, the consulate, the embassy, the ERC, or his wife put on him to give up. He *would not* leave France. He *would* continue his work right under the nose of Adolf Hitler's Gestapo. And he *would* succeed.

Varian continued to expand the work and needed more guides to take people over the border into Spain. Then he heard about a bold, daring couple named Hans and Lisa Fittko. From Berlin, the Fittkos were anti-Nazis who fought against Hitler's iron grip on their country. They stayed in Germany as long as possible, until they were hunted by the Gestapo and knew they must escape to France.

In May of 1940 Lisa Fittko, like most German Jews, had been imprisoned in a French concentration camp. She was taken to the Gurs camp, along with thousands of other women, including Marta Feuchtwanger. But Lisa refused to give in to fear and desperation, choosing instead to look for a way to get out of the camp. By the end of June she'd found it. A friend of Lisa's named Lotte worked in the office of the commandant. While looking through drawers one day, she found blank release forms. Lotte took them. These were priceless because, with the commandant's signature at the bottom, the person who was listed at the top could walk out the gate of the camp and be free. Another camp friend of Lisa's, Nelly, was experienced at forging documents. Nelly went to work perfecting the signature of the commandant, and soon no one could tell the difference. For their safety, the three women gave themselves false identities and claimed to be citizens of Belgium rather than Germany.

Using forged release forms, Lisa and about sixty other women walked out of the gate of Gurs with the permission of the guard. Included in this group, along with Lisa, Lotte, and Nelly, were Marta Feuchtwanger and Hannah Arendt, who would later become a well-known author and philosopher in America.

Lisa eventually found her husband, Hans, and in the fall of 1940 they were living in the French harbor town of Port-Vendres near the Spanish border. Like all refugees, Hans and Lisa were looking for an opportunity to escape France. They considered going over the Pyrenees, but they had been warned that the border crossing at Cerbère where the Werfels and Manns had crossed was now being watched by the border patrol and should not be used.

One day the Fittkos met Vincent Azéma, mayor of Banyuls, the town next to Cerbère. Azéma wanted to help refugees, so he told the Fittkos about a safe passage across the Pyrenees. It was an ancient smugglers' route known to the local people. This path through the mountains was much steeper and more difficult to climb, and was farther into the mountains to the west, than the one the refugees had taken from Cerbère.

Lisa had already used the smugglers' route to guide refugees over the mountains. One was Walter Benjamin, a famous German author, philosopher, and literary critic. Benjamin refused to leave behind his black leather briefcase containing the manuscript for his next book, which he believed was more important than either his discomfort or his life. In her memoir *Escape Through the Pyrenees*, Lisa Fittko wrote about the tragic trip with Walter Benjamin. It took them ten hours to go up the mountain and across the Spanish border. Then it took her two hours to come back down to Banyuls. She later learned that although she had guided Benjamin over the mountains safely, the Spanish authorities at Portbou would not allow him into Spain without an exit visa. Sure that he would never again have the strength to go over the mountain and fearful that he would be turned over to the Gestapo, Walter Benjamin committed suicide by taking an overdose of morphine. The manuscript in his briefcase vanished, never to be seen again.

Varian had heard about the Fittkos guiding refugees over the mountains and arranged to meet them. Lisa and Hans were willing to share information about the smugglers' route with Varian so that other refugees could cross the border.

Varian and Beamish met the couple at a small café just off the Old Port in Marseilles, where the salty sea breeze smelled slightly of fish. Row after row of brightly colored rowboats and sailboats were tied in the harbor. Just off the coast lay the Château d'If, the island prison made famous by Alexandre Dumas *père* in his book *The Count of Monte Cristo*.

Hans and Lisa Fittko in Marseilles.

There, in the middle of the shabby bistro on the shabby side street, the well-dressed American looked out of place.

Varian got right to the point. He didn't want the Fittkos to show him a map across the mountains. He wanted them to guide his protégés over them.

Hans and Lisa Fittko said no. They had been fighting the Nazis for years and believed the time had come to get out of Europe themselves.

Varian promised that if they guided refugees over the mountains for a while, he would help them get out of France. The Fittkos knew Varian meant what he said, but such a promise might be impossible to keep.

Since Varian didn't speak German as well as he did French, Beamish spoke to the Fittkos in German. He assured them that Varian could be trusted. Varian was listening, but misunderstood the conversation.

In her book *Escape Through the Pyrenees*, Lisa Fittko recalled what happened next:

> *"Combien?"* he [Varian] asked. "How much?"
>
> "What does he mean?" asked Hans. *"Combien* what?"
>
> *"Combien voulez-vous?"* [How much do you want?]
>
> Hans turned to Hermant [Beamish]. "Does he think we would take people across the border for money?"
>
> "Listen a moment," said Hermant. "He doesn't know you, he scarcely knows who you are. You can't expect him to understand people of the German Resistance. He's heard that racketeers are doing a booming business smuggling folks over the border; he doesn't want to deal with them. But he finds it perfectly all right if you want to be paid."

Hans regarded Fry thoughtfully. "Do you know," he said, "that assisting men of military age in illegal border-crossings now rates the death penalty? And you offer us money. We would have to be insane indeed. Do you actually know what an anti-Fascist is? Do you understand the word *Überzeugung*, convictions?"

Varian did understand the word "convictions." His convictions had made him volunteer to come to France to help when he was safe in America. His convictions had made him believe the life of each refugee was so valuable that he was willing to work sixteen hours a day to help. And his convictions had pushed him to do what was morally right, even though his actions were not legal under the Nazis' law.

The Fittkos considered what Varian was asking them to do. They had been fighting the Nazis and staying one step ahead of the Gestapo for years. Should they delay their own escape so they could help more people leave? Although tempted to refuse, Lisa and Hans Fittko would not turn their backs on others. They agreed to guide Varian's protégés over the Pyrenees Mountains.

Varian declared that the route used by the Fittkos would be called the F-Route in their honor. The Fittkos moved to Banyuls, the village close to the border. Mayor Azéma suggested that they and the refugees dress like vineyard workers going up the mountain to the fields. That way they would not look suspicious. So as not to call attention to themselves, the Fittkos decided they should take only three people over the mountains at a time.

Usually, thanks to messages delivered to them by either Maurice (Dr. Marcel Verzeano) or by Gussie Rosenberg, the Fittkos knew the names of the refugees and English soldiers who would be coming to them from Varian. However, Varian realized there would be times when sending Hans and Lisa Fittko advance warning would not be possible, so he developed a simple security system. He took a blank piece of paper and tore it in two. He sent the Fittkos one half of the paper and he kept the other half. Then, when a refugee needed to be sent unexpectedly, Varian gave that refugee his half of the torn paper. Upon arrival at the Fittkos' door, the refugee handed them Varian's torn page. If it matched their half, Hans and Lisa knew the stranger truly had been sent by Varian.

Between four and five in the morning, the refugees and either Hans or Lisa dressed as if they were going to work in the fields. In the predawn hours, no one could tell they weren't vineyard workers. If the refugees were young and healthy, they could reach the top of the rugged mountain pass in two hours (as opposed to the ten hours that it took Walter Benjamin). From there, the Fittkos pointed out to them the location of the border shack where the Spanish guards were stationed. As the refugees headed toward the Spanish border, the Fittkos returned home to Banyuls. For a period of about six months, the Fittkos guided people over the Pyrenees Mountains to the Spanish border two or three times each week.

Lisa and Hans finally left France in November 1941. By going through Cuba, they eventually came to the United States to live. Although the Fittkos never stopped to count how many, Varian estimated that they took more than one hundred people, either refugees or British soldiers, over the F-Route. The soldiers rejoined their countrymen in Gibraltar. When the refugees cleared the Spanish border, they made arrangements to travel through Spain, then through Portugal to Lisbon.

[Undercover]

SINCE LISBON, PORTUGAL, WAS NOT UNDER NAZI CONTROL, it was the departure port for most refugees fleeing Europe. Eleven thousand refugees were there, all trying to get a ticket on a ship bound for any country that wasn't dominated by the Nazis. The problem was that there were more refugees than there were places on ships.

By the end of October the Portuguese government decided it had to do something to control the number of people coming into the country. It declared it would allow in only refugees with a reserved ticket on a ship, and papers in perfect order.

This new regulation meant that every refugee needed the following documents before being allowed to enter Portugal:

A passport or "affidavit in lieu of a passport."
A visa granting permission to enter another country, such as the
   United States.
A transit visa granting permission to travel through Portugal.

> A paid-in-full ticket with a confirmed sailing date for a ship sailing
>   out of Lisbon.

It was very difficult for every member of a refugee's family to arrive at the Portuguese border before at least one of these documents
had expired. Another obstacle was that the ships leaving Lisbon announced their sailing date only four or five days before they de-
parted. This made it almost impossible for refugees to enter Portugal
with a ticket for a ship that was leaving in a couple of days.

At the same time that the new Portuguese regulations went into
effect, Spain suddenly closed its border and would not allow anyone
to enter. Then, without warning, it opened the border again for a few
hours. Then it closed it again—then reopened it again for only one
day.

Each time the Spanish border closed, Varian wondered if it would
ever open again. Everyone knew refugees had to travel through
Spain to get to Portugal, to escape Europe. Varian suspected that the
new Spanish border regulations had something to do with the visit by
Heinrich Himmler, head of the Gestapo, to Madrid. Varian worried
that the Nazis were getting ready to close in on the refugees trapped
in France. Now it would be even more difficult to get them out.

Varian redoubled his efforts. One time he paid a boat's captain to
take refugees away from Marseilles. But after the man had been paid,
he disappeared with the money and Varian found out that the boat
didn't exist. Varian still tried to find a boat that could take his protégés and some British soldiers out of Marseilles, but he wasn't successful. The police watched the port and coastline so carefully that an
escape by sea was impossible.

Once, Varian arranged to buy what he thought were genuine

Lithuanian passports, only to find out later that they were poor forgeries and that some refugees who had used them had been arrested
in Spain.

Perhaps the most costly failure came when the team paid for the
use of a phantom car. This scam occurred while Varian was trying to
find a way to get Arthur Wolff out of France. Wolff had been a Berlin
attorney who defended victims of Nazi street fights. After Hitler
came to power, Wolff and his wife fled Germany. Wolff was lame and
had to use crutches, which made it impossible for him to climb over
the Pyrenees Mountains to escape. A man who claimed he had con-
nections in Vichy offered to take five of Varian's protégés by car all
the way to Lisbon for one hundred thousand francs, which today
would be almost $34,000. Varian agreed to pay half the money up
front and the rest when the refugees arrived in Lisbon. But after the
first half of the money was paid, Varian found out that the car had
been a hoax. Eventually Maurice managed to get exit visas and Danish passports for the Wolffs, and they traveled to Cádiz, Spain, and
then on to Cuba.

Even though there were some failures, the work continued. Varian knew that as long as Hitler had a death grip on Europe, refugees
would be in danger. No matter how many people Varian could get
out of France, tens of thousands more needed help. And wouldn't the
life of the last refugee be just as valuable as the life of the first?

Because both Spain and Portugal had increased restrictions at
their borders, it was harder than ever to get refugees out of France.
That meant the ARC would need to increase its role as a relief
agency—at least until other escape routes could be worked out. More
of Varian's protégés would need to be supported financially with a
weekly allowance for food and shelter.

Varian's office would need even more people to help with the pa-

Danny Bénédite and Varian.

perwork. Mary Jayne Gold introduced Varian to an old friend of hers named Daniel Bénédite. Danny was a tall, thin, cocky Frenchman with a dimple in his chin. He had worked for the police in Paris before the war. He had been known among the refugees as one who had been helpful when many others in the police department had not been. Now in Marseilles with his British wife, Theo, he wanted to help Varian's team in any way he could.

At first Danny did only the relief work of the ARC's cover organization. But it wasn't long before he got involved in the undercover work of rescuing refugees. Danny quickly became a vital member of the team, so much so that if Varian was away from the office, Danny was in charge.

Next Varian hired a friend of Danny's, another Frenchman, named Jean Gemähling. Jean, a research chemist, was a handsome man with blond hair and blue eyes. As a boy, he'd attended an English boarding school and spoke English with just a touch of a French accent. Jean was a shy, quiet man who had a tendency to blush. In the beginning, he only interviewed refugees, but quickly he, too, got involved with Varian's underground rescue work. Beneath Jean's timid exterior was a man of great courage.

Many others worked in various capacities for Varian, including Frederic Drach, a German who sold Varian Danish and Dutch passports; Jacques Weisslitz, a Frenchman from Alsace; Paul Schmierer, a

Some of Varian's team. Left to right: Varian, Jacques Weisslitz, Theo Bénédite, Danny Bénédite, Lucie Heymann, Louis Coppermann, Marcel Verzeano, and Jean Gemähling.

doctor from Austria; Charles Wolff, a French journalist; and Berlin-born Marcel Chaminade, who was useful in dealings with Vichy authorities because he knew many of them personally.

On October 3, 1940, the French government in Vichy passed the Statute of the Jews, anti-Semitic legislation similar to the German Nuremberg Laws. Suddenly the Jews of France were forced out of their jobs and professions. Then, throughout the month, police raids became more frequent. There was no way to predict when or where one might happen. Without warning or reason, the police would start arresting everyone in sight on a street or in a café. Some of Varian's protégés were arrested in those random raids and sent to concentration camps.

Varian and his team kept a grueling schedule, officially working from 8 a.m. until 11 p.m., and sometimes until 1 a.m. Varian received anywhere from six to twelve telephone calls an hour. Twenty-five letters arrived for him each day, every one begging for help. Varian had to make countless decisions each day on how to handle the case of each refugee.

His schedule left Varian little time to write letters, but when he did, he understood that the Vichy police or Gestapo could be reading them. He wrote so that everything he said could be applied to his legal relief work. He didn't write anything that would endanger his undercover rescue work or his protégés. On October 27 he wrote to Eileen and poured out his growing frustration with the leaders of the ERC in New York. Varian's relationships with the people at the home office had been tense ever since they'd insisted he leave Marseilles and he'd refused to go. They didn't seem to understand that Varian wasn't ignoring their orders because he didn't want to go home. He

Men who worked for Varian in various capacities. On the far right is Danny Bénédite; to his left (with backs to camera) are Heinz Oppenheimer, Hans Sahl, and Marcel Chaminade. At the far left at the end of the table is Marcel Verzeano, and to his left are Frederic Drach, Paul Schmierer, and Jacques Weisslitz.

After the Germans occupied the South of France, Frederic Drach was shot to death in his hotel room. Jacques Weisslitz died in a concentration camp.

simply refused to abandon his protégés. He would not leave until someone else came to take his place.

Varian complained to his wife: "The *maddening* thing is that I get neither cooperation nor understanding from those *boobs* in New York. Our little office in the rue Grignan is keeping alive dozens of families . . . Everyone of them would have been interned if I had not come along in the nick of time. Maybe they will be anyway. *Certainly* they will be if I leave, as those blithering idiots in New York ordered me to do a month ago." Varian added, "After all, I can't stay forever. I'm tired—almost exhausted—already, and I have a wife and a job to get back to."

Continually dealing with people in crisis left Varian physically drained. He realized that if he didn't get some rest, he would become so nervous and depressed that he wouldn't be able to help the refugees. Varian said to Eileen, "I still see dozens of people every day, and am witness to displays of every possible quality of character, from heroic to despicable." Varian confessed, "It is horrible to be glad that anybody has been arrested; but I had reached a point in nervous exhaustion a few weeks ago where I actually was glad to have a few of the most insistent and most pestiferous 'clients' carried shrieking off."

When sending letters to his parents, Varian wrote to one at a time. In a letter to his mother on November 3, 1940, he gave her a glimpse into the pressure he was feeling:

Almost from the moment I arrived in Marseille I have been all but drowned in a flood of anguished human beings in search of advice and help . . . All of the time it has been like living in a crowd and being the center of it and the object of its attention . . . They begin telephoning me at half past seven in the morning, and they go right

on until eleven at night. They await me in the salon, and spring at me
when I come out of the elevator. They catch me on the streets. One or
two have even come right up to my room and walked in, without
either announcing themselves or knocking. Finally when one of my
"customers" took the room right next to mine, quite obviously in order
to get more of my time than he was entitled to, I decided things had
gone too far: I moved.

Just a few days before, Varian had moved from the hotel into a
château. The idea had been Mary Jayne Gold's. She and some of the
other staff members decided they should move out of their hotel
rooms and rent a house together. One day Mary Jayne, Miriam, and
Jean went in search of a suitable place. They took a trolley through
the suburbs to an area known as La Pomme. There they found an old
château called the Villa Air-Bel perched on the top of a hill. In her
book *Crossroads Marseilles 1940*, Mary Jayne described how it looked
the first time she saw it on that crisp autumn day:

A shady avenue led us up a gentle slope and ended on a flattened-
out area where through an iron grille we could see a graveled terrace
planted with three large and shady plane trees. The leaves had just
begun to fall and now lay about, yellow and brown on the beige
pebbles. Facing us, set back from the trees, rose the ivy-covered side
of the house. It was a great block of a building, three stories high,
topped with a low-sloping pink tile roof.

While standing on the terrace next to the house, Mary Jayne and
the others noticed that the overgrown garden below them had a fishpond with a fountain in the middle of it. Looking farther toward the
sea, they saw red tiled roofs of homes scattered between the pine,

cedar, and olive trees. In the distance lay the glittering Mediterranean Sea. The view was breathtaking.

Most of the eighteen rooms in the house were filled with furniture that had belonged to the owner's family for many years. The bedrooms had beautiful mahogany pieces and wood-burning fireplaces. The floor in the living room was covered with black-and-white tiles in a checkerboard pattern. In the upstairs library the wallpaper depicted large scenes from Greek mythology.

The Villa Air-Bel was worn and shabby in some areas, but it had an old-fashioned charm that was irresistible. Mary Jayne, Miriam, and Jean rented it and hired a cook and a maid. Immediately they called the old house "the château," even though it was not exactly a mansion. Since the house was so big, in addition to Mary Jayne, Varian, and Jean, more of the ARC staff moved in, including Danny and Theo Bénédite and their three-year-old son, Pierre. Also, Mary Jayne's black poodle, named Dagobert, and Varian's new black poodle puppy, Clovis, joined the humans. Moving to the Villa Air-Bel gave Varian some time away from the refugees in Marseilles. The villa did not have a telephone and it took about half an hour to get there by trolley.

Miriam didn't move into the house because she had finally gotten together all the papers she needed to go to her fiancé in Yugoslavia. She planned to marry him there, then work on getting them both out of Europe and to America. She ultimately succeeded.

Also invited to live at the Villa Air-Bel were a couple of the team's most famous protégés. André Breton, the founder of a style of art called Surrealism, moved in with his wife, Jacqueline, and five-year-old daughter, Aube. Writer Victor Serge, his girlfriend Laurette Séjourné, and his son, Vlady, moved in. Serge nicknamed the Villa Air-Bel the Château Espère-Visa ("house hoping for a visa").

Villa Air-Bel.

In addition to the residents, there were a number of guests. One was Walter Meyerhof. Varian had already helped his father, the Nobel Prize–winning biochemist Otto Meyerhof, out of France. Others were Max Ernst, a leader in the Dada art movement, and André Masson, a Surrealist artist. Peggy Guggenheim, a wealthy American woman who collected modern art, stayed for a time at the Villa Air-Bel. Peggy's uncle Solomon R. Guggenheim founded the Guggenheim Museum in New York City. She had inherited her wealth from her father, Benjamin, after he went down with the *Titanic* on April 15, 1912.

About the time that Varian and the others were settling in at the château, many of his protégés who had been arrested were trying to survive in various concentration camps around France. Among them were Peter Pringsheim, a physicist, Erich Itor Kahn, a pianist and

Pictured left to right: Max Ernst, Jacqueline Breton, André Masson, André Breton, and Varian Fry.

composer, and Wolf Leslau, an expert on the languages of Ethiopia. None had been imprisoned for committing a crime—they were imprisoned for being refugees.

Varian and Danny agreed that Danny would go around to the concentration camps in the South of France to find out where their protégés were held and to see the condition of the camps. They hoped that, with more information, they could persuade Vichy authorities to release their protégés. And they would also learn how they could meet the needs of these people while they were imprisoned.

By this time, early November, Varian had been away from home about three months. Back in New York, Eileen missed her husband and wanted him to return. Although she realized Varian was overworked and had little time and energy to write her, still she was hurt. In a letter to Varian dated November 10, 1940, she wrote: "If you ever feel inclined to express any interest in my welfare or any personal affection, by cable or letter, such expression would be most welcome."

Following his tour of concentration camps, Danny reported on what he'd seen. Conditions behind the barbed wire were horrific. Tens of thousands of men, women, and children were imprisoned in camps. They were hungry all the time—so hungry that even the rats scurrying around the buildings were considered a good meal. The disgusting smell of the outhouse overwhelmed the prisoners as they stood in long lines for their turn to use it. At night they slept on straw or damp sand on the floor. They lay in rows, lined up like matches in a matchbook, right next to each other. They had no privacy. They had no way to keep their bodies or their clothes clean. Many were sick with dysentery or typhus. Biting fleas, lice, and bedbugs increased their misery.

In mid-November, Danny completed his written description of French concentration camps. Varian decided that he and Marcel Chaminade would take Danny's report to Vichy. They wanted to convince the people in power that the standard of living in the camps

Men, women, and children imprisoned in a French concentration camp at Rivesaltes. The guard standing in front is a French national policeman.

should be improved. Although they didn't really expect this, Varian hoped they could get some of their protégés released from the camps. And while he was in Vichy, Varian thought he should go to the American Embassy to get some of his own travel documents in order.

With no time to write a letter, on November 16 Varian sent Eileen a short cable that said:

RETURNING SOONAS SUCCESSOR ARRIVES CANNOT LEAVE BEFORE.

When they arrived in Vichy, Varian and Marcel Chaminade arranged a meeting with the official in charge of concentration camps. As soon as the man realized they were there to complain, he became defensive.

"What is wrong with our concentration camps?" he asked. "The occupying authorities have felicitated us on them. May I ask what you find wrong with them?"

Vichy leaders had no intention of improving camp conditions. And they certainly were not going to release any of Varian's protégés. There was nothing else Varian could do in Vichy about the concentration camp problem.

Varian's next stop was the American Embassy. His French exit visa had just expired, and since he wasn't sure how much longer he would be in France, he decided he needed a Swiss visa. It was standard procedure for foreign relief workers to have a valid French exit visa and a Swiss entry visa at all times. That way, if political conditions in France got worse and put them in danger, they could immediately leave France and enter Switzerland, a neutral country. The American Embassy had already helped every other American relief worker in France to get these documents.

But the American Embassy refused to help Varian. The United

States was not involved in the war in Europe and did not know if it would ever enter the war. At this time, in 1940, the Nazis were so powerful that it seemed likely that Hitler would win the war and become supreme dictator of most of Europe.

For diplomatic reasons, the American government was trying to maintain a peaceful relationship with the French authorities who were now collaborating with the Nazis. The U.S. government certainly didn't want any problems in Vichy. And Varian was causing trouble. Vichy authorities had complained to the American Embassy about him.

The embassy wanted Varian to leave France.

"How many times do we have to tell you that we can't do anything for you?" an official at the embassy replied when Varian asked for help with his visas.

After two weeks in Vichy, Varian was disappointed that he had not accomplished anything. Returning to Marseilles, he found out that Charlie Fawcett had left France. But Charlie didn't go empty-handed. He took with him secret information, some meant for the British, some for the ERC office in New York. Since Charlie was an artist, it was natural that his bags were filled with paintings, drawings, and small sculpted heads he'd created. But inside the sculptures he'd hidden secret documents. He also hid papers inside one of the valves of his trumpet. Charlie was clever. In case anyone grew suspicious and insisted that he play his trumpet, he'd learned a few pieces that didn't use the valve where the papers were hidden.

When Charlie got to Spain, he was arrested and sent to occupied France, where he was questioned by the Gestapo. This time the language barrier helped him—he didn't speak German, and the Gestapo didn't speak English. At one point they put him in a waiting room. Since he was there alone, he just gathered up his suitcase, trumpet,

Varian Fry in his tweed suit at the Villa Air-Bel.

and bags, walked out, and jumped onto a train headed toward Madrid. Charlie succeeded in safely getting himself and all the smuggled papers through to their intended destinations.

Charlie planned to go to Britain and join the Royal Air Force, but he was sick and the air force wouldn't take him. He returned to America around the beginning of 1941. By the time he got there, he had to be hospitalized for a serious case of tuberculosis, but he slowly recovered.

Varian found time to write to his wife again on November 29, saying:

> This job is like death—irreversible. We have started something here we can't stop. We have allowed hundreds of people to become dependent upon us. We can't now say we're bored and are going home . . . I'd leave for home like a shot, you see, if I could . . . Only I simply cannot leave until my successor has arrived and worked into the job.

At the end of November a bitter cold winter settled in Marseilles, complete with snow, which was rare for the coastal city. Varian and the others at the Villa Air-Bel suffered in the freezing temperatures with colds, sore throats, and earaches. When Varian and the refugees arrived in Marseilles months before, they were all dressed for summer. Packing his bag in August, Varian had brought only a Burberry raincoat with him. Now he had to borrow an overcoat.

Supplies in Marseilles for almost everything, including shoes and clothes, were scarce. Varian hoped he could have a coat of his own made. Earlier in the month, he had written a letter to his mother that said: "I may still with luck be able to have one made, if I can find a tailor who has cloth *and* thread *and* buttons left (a rare combination)." Varian needed other clothing as well, since the few items he'd brought with him were frayed and full of holes from overuse. Varian finally found a tailor who had enough fabric to make two new suits for him. One was a salt-and-pepper tweed, and the other was a gray flannel with stripes.

[Enemies]

IN EARLY DECEMBER, VICHY LEADER PHILIPPE PÉTAIN
planned to travel through Marseilles. His coming caused the police to
want to get many refugees off the streets. On the day before he was
to arrive, Varian asked Lena to join him at Villa Air-Bel so they could
work there. Lena was late. When she got to the house, she explained
that she and many refugees had been arrested. After checking her papers, the police had released her.

Varian decided that they should work awhile that morning, and
he would see what he could do to have his protégés released in the afternoon. He was in the middle of dictating a letter to Lena when the
police pulled up to the château. They had brought with them a paddy
wagon big enough to hold all the occupants of the Villa Air-Bel.

The maid knocked at Varian's door and told him and Lena that
the police were downstairs. But Varian wanted to finish dictating the
letter before going to them.

A few minutes later, Victor Serge came to Varian's door to tell
him that the police wanted everyone in the hall downstairs. Varian

looked around the room, his eyes now trained to detect anything that could be used against him. His address book, full of names, addresses, and notes about money transactions, lay on the table. He knew he couldn't let the information contained in the book fall into the hands of the police. Varian regretted losing all the information he had carefully gathered, but he knew what must be done. He tossed the book into the fireplace and watched the flames eat up its secrets.

Downstairs, four plainclothes policemen said they'd come to search the house for anything that could link its inhabitants with Communist activities. Apparently they knew that both André Breton and Victor Serge had been members of the Communist Party. One by one, a policeman took each person in the house upstairs to search his or her room while the rest waited downstairs with the other officers. When André Breton's room was being searched, it occurred to Varian that there was a forged passport in his own, lying with some books on his dresser. He had to get up there and hide it before the police searched his room, and he had to do it fast.

He asked the police captain if he might be allowed to use the toilet. The captain said he could go, but sent a police officer to wait in the hall for him. Walking up the stairs, Varian made friendly small talk with the officer. In the bathroom, Varian stalled for time. How could he get into his room alone long enough to hide the fake passport? Suddenly it came to him. He flushed the toilet and walked into the hall.

"I just have to get a handkerchief. I'll be right back," said Varian casually, and moved toward his room.

He was relieved when the officer stood where he was and didn't make a move to follow him.

In a flash, Varian grabbed the fake passport and threw it on top of the wardrobe. It was all he had time to do. He took a handkerchief out of the dresser drawer and walked out. Varian blew his nose to complete the ruse.

In *Surrender on Demand*, Varian described what happened after he joined Lena downstairs:

> "Engage that guy in conversation," I whispered. "I want a chance to go through my pockets."
>
> "*Entendu* [understood]," she said. "But when you finish, I want a chance to go through my pocketbook."
>
> "All right," I said. "I'll do what I can."

Since only one policeman was left in the room with them, Lena distracted him by complimenting his blue pinstripe suit. Meanwhile, Varian cleaned out his pockets and threw the papers into the wood-burning stove along with a log. Then it was Varian's turn to distract the man so Lena could go through her purse. Lena nonchalantly stoked the fire in the stove as the evidence against her turned to ash.

When the police were finished with their search, they had found and confiscated two revolvers, one from Victor Serge and the other from André Breton. They also took with them two typewriters and all the papers on Varian's desk. The police took into custody everyone except for the maid, the cook, the children, Pierre and Aube, and their mothers, Theo Bénédite and Jacqueline Breton. As Varian and the others rode together in the back of the police paddy wagon, they assumed they'd been picked up for assisting refugees.

They were kept at the police station for the rest of the day. Around midnight, they were taken to a ship, the SS *Sinaia*. Coincidentally, it was the same ship on which Varian had sailed to Europe during his college days. This stay was a little different. Varian, his staff, and about six hundred other people were held there for more than three days. They were relieved to realize that the police had swept through the city in a massive raid and had temporarily arrested about twenty thousand people in Marseilles. All were being detained out of sight to clear the streets and prevent any problems while Pétain was in the city. The arrests had nothing to do with any illegal activities.

Yet after this incident the police followed Varian closely. Varian knew they were shadowing him, so he was cautious about whom he talked to and where he went. He wrote that after about two weeks they "got tired of learning where I had lunch and dinner every day and called the whole thing off. But as long as it lasted it was uncomfortable enough."

Then one day in the middle of December the police came to Varian's office looking for Albert Hirschman. Beamish happened to be out of town, but Varian told the police he no longer worked at the office. Now that the police were looking for him, Beamish was not safe in Marseilles any longer. Varian knew he had to leave.

When Beamish got back to the city, he said his goodbyes. The Fittkos guided him over the Pyrenees.

Although Varian had known Beamish for only about four months, the nature of their work had forged a strong bond between them. Beamish had been the first member of Varian's team, and he was the only other person who knew absolutely everything about Varian's work. Varian wrote: "With Beamish and Beamish alone I could be perfectly candid and natural. After he left I was completely alone, and I felt my solitude as I had never felt it before." But the work had to go on, both the undercover effort to get the refugees safely out of France and the relief services provided by the American Relief Center.

As members of the original team escaped Marseilles, Varian had to replace them at the ARC office. He decided that the new people who were hired would never know anything about his underground work. Everyone in the office would believe that Varian simply ran an American relief organization for refugees. This way, if they were ever questioned by the police, they could honestly deny that anything illegal was going on at the ARC. It would be safer for them, safer for Varian, and safer for the protégés. So from this time on, only a few people, including Danny, Jean, Maurice, Gussie, Mary Jayne, and Lena, knew that Varian was secretly making arrangements to smuggle refugees out of France.

Varian's undercover work caused him to clash again and again with the authorities of the United States. In response to the refugee crisis in Europe, the United States was willing to grant visas allowing some refugees into the country—but only a very limited number. America was still trying to recover from the Great Depression of the 1930s. Most Americans did not want to take in millions of European refugees when they themselves were trying to find a way to support their families.

But Varian believed helping refugees out of Europe was the right thing to do. And when Varian thought he was right, he was willing to battle anyone and everyone who stood against him. In the four months he'd been in Marseilles, Varian had made some enemies. And not all of them were Nazis or Vichy policemen—many were American Foreign Service officials. No one in the American Foreign Service liked Varian, with the exception of Harry Bingham, the vice-consul in Marseilles who had helped Lion Feuchtwanger escape from the concentration camp.

Varian had always freely shared his thoughts and opinions with other people. Now that the lives of refugees hung in the balance, he was fearless as he fought to save some of them. Varian did not think the State Department in Washington, D.C., the American Embassy in Vichy, and the American Consulate in Marseilles were doing enough to help refugees get visas. He had frequent disagreements with American officials as he relentlessly pushed them to grant more visas. Varian sent them so many letters and messages asking for American visas that they began to refer to all communications from him as "Fryanna."

It didn't matter to Varian how the American officials felt about him; what mattered was getting refugees to safety. He was willing to give one hundred percent of his energy as he pushed American officials to grant more visas. Varian understood that every American visa granted meant one less refugee in the hands of the Nazis.

Varian was fighting for the lives of as many refugees as he could save, but the number of European refugees was staggering. *The New York Times* reported on December 15, 1940:

> Very little is now being done about the main mass of refugees still in the occupied countries. Refugee officials here estimated today the racial and political refugees in various countries at 1,500,000 in Poland, 240,000 in Germany, 80,000 in Czecho-Slovakia, 1,000,000 in Hungary, 400,000 in Rumania, 60,000 in Italy, 100,000 in France and the same number in Spain.
>
> In France alone there are 40,000 in camps, but very few of these refugees can even get transit visas to come to this last port of exile from Europe [Lisbon].

Varian had understood long before most people that the Jews were in real danger. Perhaps it was because he'd witnessed Nazi brutality against Jews on the street in Berlin five years before. For the rest of the world, it was harder to comprehend. Yet the public could read in newspapers about the cold, calculated methods of terror the Nazis used on the Jews. On December 17, a *New York Times* article described what was happening in Alsace, an area in northeastern France that had been annexed by Germany:

> By a decree issued in Strasbourg, German-occupied Alsace, by Reich Statthalter Robert Wagner, the property of Jews is confiscated and will be distributed either gratis or at low prices to necessitous Alsatian evacuees, who, on returning to their homes have found them destroyed or damaged during the hostilities.
>
> Houses belonging to Jews have been sold at "auction"—attended solely by German immigrants who are told in advance for which properties they may bid and how much to bid for them . . .
>
> The finer furnishings contained in the seized buildings have been sent to Germany by the trainload; ceremonious distribution of such things as kitchen implements and furnishings occurs frequently in the public places to the necessitous "Aryans," who have had enough foresight to join the [Nazi] party ranks.
>
> The Mulhouse Tageblatt [newspaper] said: ". . . This distribution is only just, since the Jews only acquired these belongings by exploiting the down-trodden worker and moreover they are the ones principally responsible for the war."
>
> . . . Vans of youths arrive in the dead of night and calmly inform tenants of the richer farms they have but a few minutes to leave; they leave.

Sadly, this was happening everywhere. Whenever Nazis conquered an area, all Jewish property was confiscated.

Varian didn't know how much longer he would be in France.

He'd received a cable from the home office that said his successor was on the way—but not who he would be or when he would arrive. Varian was ready to go home just as soon as his replacement had settled in and understood all areas of the work. But until then Varian planned to work as hard as he could.

Refugees continued to line up each day at the ARC. Varian and his staff interviewed fifty refugees a day. They continued to add names to the list of protégés they were trying to get out of France. But most of the refugees they interviewed were given general aid such as meal tickets and help with letters and applications for foreign visas. During the previous month, November, the ARC office sent out 470 letters on behalf of refugees. They would send more than that in December.

One day in the middle of December, Varian got an unusual message asking him to meet a "friend" at the Hôtel Splendide. When he arrived, he found a young man and a middle-aged woman waiting. Jay Allen and Margaret Palmer had arrived in Marseilles to take over for Varian. Allen, a journalist, handed Varian a letter from the ERC that terminated Varian as its representative in Marseilles.

Allen declared he would run things from behind the scenes. He himself would never go to the office, and he did not intend to meet any of the staff face-to-face. Palmer, who came from the Carnegie Institute of Art, would take Varian's place in the office. The plan was that Palmer would keep Allen informed about everything, then Allen would issue his instructions to Palmer. Palmer would relay his messages to the others.

Allen explained to Varian that he would continue his work as a journalist for the North American Newspaper Alliance. He hoped to go to Vichy and obtain an interview with Pétain, France's leader.

Right away Varian felt that Allen wasn't interested in the work at all. He planned to do Varian's job in his "spare time."

Varian couldn't believe what he was hearing. He worked from sixteen to eighteen hours a day, and Jay Allen thought he could do it in his spare time. Varian was disgusted. The men disliked each other immediately.

Varian was supposed to leave Marseilles as soon as he'd trained Margaret Palmer. He had been officially relieved of duty by the home office of the Emergency Rescue Committee.

Palmer moved into Varian's office. He explained to her everything that he'd been doing, both the legal relief work and the illegal rescue work. Since some refugees and protégés were artists, Varian thought Palmer's background in art would be helpful. He wanted a successful transition of leadership from himself to Palmer and Allen. But he wasn't sure if his team would ever accept Margaret Palmer as their leader. They knew that Jay Allen would be telling Palmer what to do, but the staff would never see him. The job was difficult enough when everyone was in the same place at the same time.

Two famous refugees whose names were on Varian's original lists, artist Henri Matisse and author André Gide, had not responded to Varian's offer to help them out of France. So right before Christmas, Palmer traveled with Varian and Maurice to Nice. They went there to convince Matisse and Gide that they should leave. Both refused to go.

At the end of the year, the lease would expire on the rented space that had been supplied to the ARC by the leather merchant. Now that fifteen people were working in the office, they needed more room. They moved to 18 Boulevard Garibaldi.

Jay Allen wanted Varian to leave as soon as possible. On January 2, 1941, Allen wrote in a note to Varian:

I assume that you are making preparations to leave, with the clear understanding that your work here will be carried on to the best of my ability, without however doing it *necessarily* in your way and, if possible, expanding it in other directions.

But Varian had serious doubts about both Allen and Palmer. On January 5 Varian wrote Eileen: "I don't know what to do: whether to stay or to leave. The Friend [Jay Allen] advises me to leave immediately, but as you probably know, I have very little respect for the Friend's intelligence." As for Palmer, ever since she returned from the trip to Nice, she had been sick, which caused Varian to doubt that Palmer could handle the job: "I wonder whether, in view of her somewhat advanced age and delicate health, she can keep all of it going full steam, especially as it has always been a little too much even for husky healthy me."

Varian knew his passport would expire on January 22, so he went to the American Consulate in Marseilles to renew it. But instead of renewing Varian's passport, the consul confiscated it. He assured Varian that his passport would be returned when he was ready to go back to the United States. The consul hoped this would pressure Varian into leaving France, es-

Seventeen-year-old Justus Rosenberg (Gussie) at the center desk in the office of the American Relief Center on Boulevard Garibaldi in 1941.

pecially now that Jay Allen had arrived. It did increase the pressure on Varian, by putting him in even greater danger than before. If something happened and Varian needed to leave France suddenly, he would not be permitted out of the country, because, without a valid passport, his papers would not be in order.

What the consul didn't understand was that Varian was willing to leave France. He wanted very much to go home. He had repeatedly asked the ERC to send a replacement for him so that he could. Varian thought that when his successor arrived and learned about the work, he could return to the United States knowing that his protégés would be well cared for. But Varian knew that Jay Allen was not the right man for the job. Varian could not in good conscience leave his trusting protégés in that man's hands. Their safety was more important to him than his own desire to go home.

Varian determined not to leave his protégés to Allen, and continued to work as if Allen were not there. In fact, Allen *wasn't* there, since he spent most of his time away from Marseilles. So throughout January the office got even busier. Seven women on the staff typed one letter after another all day on behalf of the refugees, totaling 830 letters in January. Varian had no doubt that the system he'd established would fall apart if Allen took over.

Somehow Varian had to make the home office of the Emergency Rescue Committee understand why Jay Allen was not qualified to take over for him. On January 21 Varian wrote that Allen had "not had time—or apparently, interest—to listen to what I have learned." Varian told them that he had created

an organization which is known all over free France as the one hope of the refugees. I do not wish to see that organization dropped. I do not propose to leave it until I am satisfied it is in the hands of competent successors who will carry it on in something of the spirit in which I have conducted it. Jay is not that person. He is altogether too impatient, too bossy, too unwilling to listen to others or to benefit by the experience—often painful and costly—of others.

Varian complained that Allen had "not once asked what the weekly budget of this office is, how we raise the money, or how far ahead we have to keep. He has, in fact, shown no interest in the office whatever."

Since Varian refused to leave, he felt that the ERC would have to choose between them. He began to think that even if they chose Allen, he still wouldn't go. He'd come to believe that the work in Marseilles no longer belonged completely to the ERC. After all, Mary Jayne Gold continually donated large sums of money to the work. So Varian decided that if he had to, he would cut all ties with the ERC and find a way to go on without them.

Varian explained that

this office is not your office: it is an independent committee consisting of various American citizens residing in France. It has received funds from many sources, including some very substantial sums from certain American citizens residing here. As the president and director of the committee, I have no right to turn over its direction to a person in whose judgment I have not complete confidence.

The answer from the ERC was a cable on February 2, 1941, that told Varian and Jay Allen to agree upon a plan for the work there. In the middle of it all, Margaret Palmer gave up and returned home.

Between the struggle for control and his nonstop work schedule, Varian was exhausted. He wrote his mother on February 3, 1941:

I've never had a job which tired me as this one does. I think it is because of the vast numbers of people I see—forty or fifty a day at times . . . You get so tired at times that you can no longer keep your mind on what people are saying to you. You have to take notes during the conversation to force your attention upon it. And every one who comes to see you starts a whole train of things you have to do.

On February 15 Varian wrote Eileen that

this afternoon Mr. J. A. made his first, and, I hope, only visit to our office. I don't know what to think of him, he talks so much and listens so little—and you know how uninclined I am to shout people down. He said he would like to break my neck. I have no idea why . . . He said he had never hated anyone so much in his life, that I was slippery and dishonest . . . that I was "washed up," that he would "show me."

Varian would not hand over to Jay Allen the work it had taken him months to develop. Varian determined that it was Allen who would be "washed up."

[Betrayed]

MANY OF VARIAN'S STAFF AND HIS SUPPORTERS IN Europe wrote letters on his behalf, asking the ERC to let Varian continue his work. Finally, at the end of February, Varian won the battle for control. Jay Allen left Marseilles.

When Allen crossed over into the Nazi-occupied zone of France without permission, hoping he could get an interview with the head of the Vichy government, Philippe Pétain, he was arrested by the Germans. Allen stayed in prison until the end of the summer. Then he was exchanged for a German journalist who had been arrested in America. Varian admitted in a letter to Eileen that when he heard about Jay Allen's arrest, "Naturally I was kinda pleased, secretly: it was too perfect an end for a boasting, blustering fool."

As the bitter cold winter dragged on, there was a shortage of coal for the stoves both at home and at the office. At the Villa Air-Bel, the only way to obtain any warmth at all was to take wood from the surrounding trees. But most of the wood had to be used for cooking in the château's woodstove. The bedrooms were so cold at night that

Varian and his staff put their coats on top of the covers for an extra layer of warmth.

Not only were they all cold, they were hungry, too. There was not enough food to adequately feed the people in France. The Germans had taken most of it for themselves. What was left was rationed out. It was common to see a line two people deep and two blocks long snaking out the door of a butcher shop. Then, after standing in line for hours, many walked away empty-handed when the meat was gone. Meat became so scarce that a slice of horsemeat was considered a treat. Some people killed cats and sold them as rabbit.

At the Villa Air-Bel there was never enough to eat. Meals consisted mainly of boiled Jerusalem artichokes and boiled squash. Occasionally there was a small helping of spaghetti or macaroni, without any sauce. Every now and then the cook was able to obtain a few wrinkly, bruised apples, which were devoured with joy.

For a while, the staff had been able to keep hidden a cow that provided milk for Aube Breton and Pierre Bénédite, the children in the house. The milk was also shared with children in the surrounding area. Then one day the cow was discovered and her milk had to be given over to the city authorities.

The staff even ate the goldfish they scooped out of the fishpond. On Sundays, Varian and Danny hunted snails in the garden and put them in burlap bags to dry. After the snails dried, they were boiled and eaten. To feed the dogs, Varian and Mary Jayne asked local restaurants for their scraps.

Even bread was scarce. The cook had to weigh portions on a scale so that each person got an equal part. The tiny portions were placed on plates at breakfast. Every morning there was a choice to make: either eat all of your bread at breakfast, or eat a little bit and save some for dinner.

Varian and his housemates were sometimes so hungry they couldn't sleep. In the middle of the long nights, the temptation to sneak into the kitchen to get just a small morsel of the next day's bread ration was strong. The cook had to lock the bread cupboard at night. In a letter to Eileen on March 18, Varian wrote: "We are all hungry here all the time . . . and dream of cakes and cookies. If you send us anything, send us sugar and sweets and fats. Also soap."

By the end of April even the bread was gone. Varian, a thin man already, had lost twenty pounds.

As soon as possible in the spring, the Villa Air-Bel housemates planted a vegetable garden around the fishpond. Eventually it helped supplement their meals. On May 14 Varian wrote his father that he dreamed of "beefsteaks, mashed potatoes with butter, and ice cream."

Despite being constantly hungry and cold, Varian loved living in

The fishpond at Villa Air-Bel on November 3, 1940. Varian is bent over in the water; standing in the background on the right is André Breton; standing on the left is Victor Serge. The others cannot be identified.

One of the art auctions held at the Villa Air-Bel. Varian is standing on the far right in the white shirt and tie; André Breton is holding a stick in his two hands; Breton's wife, Jacqueline, is the woman on the right wearing the white blouse and long necklace.

the old château. For him, the best part of the Villa Air-Bel was the company of the fascinating people who lived and visited there. Even though the housemates differed in life experience and political ideals, they bonded against the Nazis, their common enemy. At night they gathered to discuss the war and what was happening in the world, sometimes arguing with each other. They took their minds off their hunger by singing songs and playing games. Mary Jayne recalled one game they called "Murder." The designated assassin was given a piece of paper on which the name of the victim was written. The players turned out the lights and moved around. Then the victim was tapped on the shoulder, and he or she screamed and fell to the floor. When the lights came on, the players stayed where they were, and the investigation to find the assassin began.

Because Surrealist artists André Breton, Max Ernst, and André Masson were staying at the Villa Air-Bel, other Surrealist artists such as Óscar Domínguez, Benjamin Péret, Wifredo Lam, and Victor Brauner came to the château to visit. On Sundays, this group of talented artists gathered on the terrace with the entire household. They hung art from the branches of the plane trees and held art auctions.

During this time, Hans Sahl, one of Varian's first protégés, was at last able to escape France. Sahl had worked at Varian's office while they looked for a way to get him out of the country. He was one of the many stateless Germans who no longer had a valid passport. With a forged passport from Denmark, Sahl crossed the French-Spanish border and made his way through Spain. He wrote about leaving France in his book *The Few and the Many*:

> In my suitcase were a great many little slips of paper with news from Occupied France—I hid them in toothpaste tubes and cans of shoe polish. Among other things I had the list drawn up by the Germans at the Hôtel Splendide, the names of the persons who were to be surrendered to them. When I arrived in Madrid I went, according to instructions, up to a porter wearing a certain number, gave him my suitcase, and said some password I've since forgotten. The porter nodded and took my suitcase over to a little horse-drawn carriage waiting by the station. I got into the carriage and was driven to a small pension on a quiet street. No one asked my name.

The next day Sahl took the train to Lisbon. From there he sailed first to Martinique, then to the United States. With the names of refugees who were on the Gestapo's list that he'd smuggled out of Europe, Sahl arrived safely in New York.

Then, without any explanation, Vichy began to grant more French exit visas. It made Varian think that the Gestapo had decided which refugees they wanted to find. As for all the rest, Vichy and the Germans evidently wanted to get rid of as many as possible. Armed with exit visas, more refugees were able to escape France.

Suddenly ships were allowed to sail directly from Marseilles to the Caribbean island of Martinique, a French territory. The long-hoped-for chance to get refugees out of France by sea was finally a reality. With only a French exit visa, refugees could now sail to Martinique directly from Marseilles, and from there make arrangements to go to America or any other country that would allow them in.

Through the late winter and spring of 1941, Varian's staff, which numbered twenty at this point, was busier than ever. They all worked long hours arranging passage by ship for their protégés. One refugee left by ship in February; a few more in early March; twenty-five at the end of March; and twelve more a week later. During the rest of April and May, sometimes as many as ninety at a time left on one ship.

In April, 1941, Vichy police arrested all Jews who were staying in Marseilles hotels. Some of Varian's protégés were picked up, including Marc Chagall, who had been on Varian's original ERC list. Months before, he'd contacted Chagall about leaving France, but the world-famous painter hadn't wanted to leave. He didn't think he

Varian Fry, Marc Chagall, his wife, Bella Chagall, and Harry Bingham, at the Chagalls' home in Gordes.

would be in danger and didn't want to interrupt his work. Varian even went to see him at his home in Gordes to convince him.

Now that the Vichy government had instituted anti-Jewish laws, however, Chagall decided he must escape. He and his wife had traveled to Marseilles so they could leave France. They had been there only a short time when Marc Chagall was arrested during one of the hotel raids.

Varian was in the office when he answered the telephone call from a frantic Mrs. Chagall, who reported her husband's arrest. Varian immediately called the police station. He told the policeman that if the world found out that Vichy police had arrested the world-famous artist Marc Chagall, the government would be deeply embarrassed.

Varian got off the phone and told Danny, "If he isn't out in half an hour, we'll call up the *New York Times* and give them the news."

Within thirty minutes Marc Chagall was back at his hotel. He and his wife were among the fortunate protégés who safely made their way to the United States. Some of Varian's protégés who were arrested in the hotel raids were not so lucky. They were sent to concentration camps.

During the first few months of 1941, many famous refugees escaped from France. Besides Marc Chagall, they included Max Ernst, Jacques Lipchitz, Hans Sahl, André Breton, André Masson, Victor Serge, and Walter Mehring.

While Varian was getting refugees out of France, things weren't going so well back home. His employer back in New York had been holding his job for him. But the Foreign Policy Association couldn't hold it any longer. So Varian didn't have a job to go back to. And during January and February, when he was feuding with Jay Allen and refusing to leave, the ERC had not paid his salary. Then the ERC decided to cut Varian's salary in half.

Also, the distance between Varian and his wife was growing. Varian wrote to Eileen about the possibility that she might join him in France, but that never happened. During his extended absence, Eileen had lost fifteen pounds from stress. She was caught in the tension between Varian and the leaders of the ERC office, and she tried to be a peacemaker between them. She worried about Varian, and the fact that she got few letters from him made matters worse. At one point she closed a letter with "Much love if you're interested."

By then Eileen knew that Varian would be staying in France for as long as he could. She had no idea how long that might be. Later she wrote: "Miss you badly . . . If you are not coming back, write me some practical details about living expenses and plans, etc. Your latest cable, after all, says you're 'planning to stay indefinitely.' "

Yet no matter how difficult circumstances were for Varian, he knew they were much worse for the Jews of Europe. By the beginning of May, many French citizens were turning against the Jews. Varian wrote Eileen on May 3, 1941: "The anti-semitism of France is not just official any more, either. It is beginning to take hold of the people. Apparently it is the easiest virus to spread in any country . . . There are also anti-semitic posters which attract attention and approval of crowds."

At the end of May, Varian and his staff compiled statistics about their work. In *Surrender on Demand*, Varian reported that in less than eight months more than 15,000 people had either come to their office or written them. The ARC had to decide whether or not it could help each one. Out of the 15,000, they took on 1,800 as protégés. Since most of those 1,800 had families, Varian actively worked on behalf of around 4,000 people. The ARC had paid weekly living allowances to 560 families, and helped them in all sorts of ways, from buying them clothes to getting them a dentist. Over 1,000 people, including some protégés and their families, had gotten out of France. Other protégés had been sent to concentration camps, and Varian had tried to get them released. When that was unsuccessful, the ARC helped by sending them food packages, which occasionally Gussie would deliver.

Since the early days of his work, Varian had depended on getting access to the protégés' money through the exchange system set up by Beamish. As the months passed, the gangsters in Marseilles continued to find people who wanted to exchange their local cash for U.S. dollars, which would be deposited in a bank in America. Varian's dealings with the gangsters had been successful so far, and he trusted his contact.

The contact was a Russian whom Varian called Dimitru in *Surrender on Demand*, where Varian changed several names. Dimitru's real name was Kurrillo. Varian wrote that Dimitru "was less than five feet tall, had manners which were extravagantly polite, and a right hand which felt like an empty glove when you shook it. He could turn his smile on and off like an electric light." Dimitru acted as an intermediary between the client and Varian. When the money was exchanged, Dimitru took a percentage of the transaction as his payment.

In the spring of 1941 Dimitru offered Varian the chance to buy for $8,000 some gold that would be worth $15,000 in U.S. dollars. Varian made the deal. When he took possession of the gold, he immediately buried it beneath the pine trees at the Villa Air-Bel. Not long after, the police came to the château with a warrant to search for gold and foreign money. They didn't find the gold, but the timing made Varian suspicious.

Then, a week later, Dimitru suggested that Varian sell half of the gold to take advantage of the favorable exchange rate. Varian agreed and made plans to bring the gold to him the next day. But Varian was busy and sent Danny in his place.

Since the gold was so heavy, Danny knew it would take two trips to carry it in his briefcase. He delivered the first case of gold to Dimitru without any problems. But when Danny walked down the street with the second load of gold in his case, he saw Dimitru standing in front of the hotel. And he noticed three men standing across the street. Danny felt something wasn't right and decided to walk past Dimitru without a word.

But instead of ignoring him, as Danny thought he would, Dimitru came down the steps and said, "I don't like the look of things just now . . . Better not bring that stuff in now. Take it back to the house. I'll see you later." Then he reached for Danny's hand and gave it a weak shake. He turned and disappeared into the building.

As the three men came toward him, Danny knew that Dimitru had double-crossed him and that he was in trouble.

The three men were Vichy police officers. They looked into Danny's case and arrested him, because it was against the law in Vichy France to have any gold. When they interrogated Danny, he made up a story that Max Ernst had given him the gold as a gift to the ARC. He took full responsibility for having the gold and swore that Varian Fry knew nothing about it. The police locked Danny up in the Prison Chave.

Varian was worried sick. Not only had Danny become second-in-command at the ARC, but he was a close personal friend. Varian knew that if Danny hadn't taken the blame, he, too, would have been arrested. Varian wrote:

Twice a day, on my way to and from the office, I passed the Prison Chave, and I thought of Danny, down there at the bottom of one of the narrow shafts of light the long prison windows must let through. And, knowing that it was I who had put him there, I wanted to go to the police and tell them to arrest me instead. But I knew that if I did the committee would immediately be closed, and hundreds of poor devils would lose their last chance to escape from the Nazis. But it would have been much easier to do that than what I had to do.

Varian got Danny a lawyer, who suspected that Danny could be convicted and sentenced to four or five years in prison. But he thought that if the American consul spoke on Danny's behalf, maybe they would make him pay a huge fine instead of going to prison.

Varian went to the consul in Marseilles to ask him to help Danny. Since the consul didn't like Varian, he was surprised and relieved when the man agreed to speak to the police on Danny's behalf. The consul went to the Vichy police and told them that because Danny worked for an American relief organization, the consulate was following his case. As a result, Danny was set free on bail to await his trial instead of being kept in prison.

When Danny came out of prison after ten days, he was filthy, skinny, and pale. Varian was so relieved to see Danny that he hugged him and wept. Varian wrote: "I felt like an awful fool . . . but I couldn't help it."

After being double-crossed by Dimitru, the ARC never got its money back. Dimitru claimed that the police had confiscated it. But the lawyer could find no record of this at the police station. The lawyer became convinced that Dimitru was working with the police, and then also learned that Dimitru was a Gestapo agent.

It was clear to Varian that they needed to get rid of Dimitru, so Varian came up with a plan to scare him off. Varian went to another gangster, a business partner of Dimitru's, and told him that he wanted to hire him to kill Dimitru. Varian knew the two were in business together and that this man would not kill his own partner in crime. And Varian never intended that Dimitru be killed—he just wanted to get him away from Marseilles. It worked. Dimitru left town and never came back.

After Danny's arrest and subsequent release, the police arrived frequently to search the house and office. Danny believed the police were trying to find some proof that Varian was breaking the law so they could deport him from France. They hesitated to kick him out without a good excuse because they did not want any bad publicity in the United States. Varian later described their tactics: "arrests, searches of the house and the office, the spreading of alarming rumors about what might happen to me if I stayed (sudden disappearance, body found in harbor several days later, for instance)—all this obviously designed to scare me out of the country." Varian was calm on the outside, but the frequent searches were making him nervous.

He was also tired of being pressured by the American Embassy and the State Department to leave. The consul in Marseilles had his passport and still refused either to renew it or to return it to him. He told Varian: "My instructions are to renew it only for immediate return to the United States, and then only for a period of two weeks."

In America, Eileen worked on his behalf by asking the First Lady of the United States to help Varian gain permission to stay in France. Eleanor Roosevelt's answer to Eileen on May 13, 1941, was that "there is nothing I can do for your husband. I think he will have to come home because he has done things which the government does not feel it can stand behind."

In June the United States instituted new policies on visas issued to refugees. Because of the new rules, even fewer refugees would be able to get American visas.

[Expelled]

IT SEEMED THAT EVERYTHING WAS CHANGING, INCLUD-
ing Villa Air-Bel. Ever since Varian had managed to get the Surrealist artists and their families away to America, the charming old
château seemed quiet, almost lifeless. The days of fascinating discus-
sions among some of the world's most talented people, the games,
and the feelings of camaraderie were gone. Now the few staff members still living there seemed to disagree constantly.

Although Varian was ready to go home, Danny and the rest of the
team believed that if Varian left, the organization would fall apart.
They also suspected they might all be arrested. Varian wondered
what would happen if he left. Would his team be in danger? What
would happen to his protégés? He decided to stay as long as he could
and leave only if a reliable replacement took over.

Eileen's frustration with Varian seemed to be growing. On July 8,
1941, she wrote to him complaining that she had not had a letter from
him in six weeks. She was also beginning to wonder what life would
be like when he did eventually come home. "I hope you are not going
to come back with my mother's habit of turning all American prices

into francs, and fainting on the spot," she wrote. She ended the letter by saying, "Please don't wait six weeks before writing."

Varian didn't know it yet, but his time in Marseilles was running out. In July the American consul warned him that the Gestapo had told the Vichy police to arrest him. A couple of days later, Varian was "invited" to meet with the head of police in Marseilles. It was clear that if Varian refused this invitation, he would be arrested.

After making Varian wait for a while, Maurice Anne Marie de Rodellec du Porzic had Varian brought to his office. The bright morning light streamed through the window behind the policeman, putting his face in shadow. Without saying a word, he opened the thick dossier that lay on his desk.

Slowly de Rodellec du Porzic looked through Varian's file, as if he had all the time in the world. He considered each page before turning to the next. From the other side of the desk, Varian recognized the stationery from his own office and realized some of his own letters were in the file.

In *Surrender on Demand*, Varian wrote about this meeting with de Rodellec du Porzic:

"You have caused my good friend the Consul-General of the United States much annoyance," he said.

"I guess the Consul can take care of his own problems," I said.

"My friend the Consul-General tells me that your government and the American committee you represent have both asked you to return to the United States without delay," he continued.

"There's some mistake," I said. "My instructions are to stay."

"This affair of your secretary," de Rodellec du Porzic went on, obviously referring to Danny, "will have very serious consequences for you."

"I can't see how," I said. "One of my employees has committed an indiscretion. But he acted entirely on his own responsibility. There is no proof that I was involved in any way."

"In the new France, we do not need proof," de Rodellec du Porzic said. "In the days of the Republic, it used to be believed that it was better to let a hundred criminals escape than to arrest one innocent man. We have done away with all that. We believe that it is better to arrest a hundred innocent men than to let one criminal escape."

"I see," I said, "that we are very far apart in our ideas of the rights of man."

"Yes," de Rodellec du Porzic said, "I know that in the United States you still adhere to the old idea of human rights. But you will come to our view in the end. It is merely a question of time. We have realized that society is more important than the individual. You will come to see that, too."

He paused to close the dossier.

"When are you leaving France?" he asked.

I said I had no definite plans.

"Unless you leave France of your own free will," he said, "I shall be obliged to arrest you and place you in *résidence forcée* [house arrest] in some small town far from Marseille, where you can do no harm."

I had to play for time.

"I see," I said. "Can you give me a little time to arrange my affairs and get someone over from America to take my place as president of the committee before I go? I'm willing to go myself, since you insist; but I want to make sure the committee will go on after I leave."

"Why are you so much interested in your committee?" he asked.

"Because it is the only hope of many of the refugees," I said.

"I see," he said. "How much time do you need?"

"Well," I said, "I'll cable New York today. It will take them a little time to find someone to replace me, and some more time for him to get his passport and visas and get here. Can you give me until the 15th of August?"

"That will be satisfactory," he said.

I got up to go. Then I turned back and asked a final question.

"Tell me," I said, "frankly, why are you so much opposed to me?"

"Parce que vous avez trop protégé des juifs et des anti-Nazis," he said. "Because you have protected Jews and anti-Nazis."

Vichy police captain de Rodellec du Porzic was right that Varian had protected Jews and anti-Nazis. And Varian would continue to do so as long as he was in France. Varian knew that no replacement for him would arrive by August 15. At least he had bought himself a little more time in France.

A couple of days later, the American consul returned Varian's passport. It had been renewed, but *only* for one month, and *only* for travel west, toward the United States. Varian was surprised to find in his passport all the documents he would need to get back to America: a French exit visa, a Spanish transit visa, and a Portuguese transit visa.

Varian went to the American Embassy in Vichy to ask for permission to stay on in France. He thought that if the embassy requested that he be allowed to stay, the French would let him.

The embassy refused.

Varian knew there was nothing else he could do. He was being forced out of France.

Varian was in Vichy when he finally answered Eileen's letter complaining that she seldom heard from him. On July 31, 1941, he wrote:

Remember that . . . I have been working very hard for two years
without vacation, and that during the past twelve months I have
worked harder than I ever have before in my life, endured more
emotional strain (hysterical refugees) and encountered almost
insuperable obstacles (to say nothing of the atmosphere of
suspicion, pressure, provocation, etc., under which I have worked and
which has at times made me rather nervous). The truth is that I
simply don't have an ounce of energy left when I get home at night;
and I can't dictate my letters to you at the office.

Varian decided to stay away from Marseilles for a time. He believed the police were watching him and waiting for a chance to expel
him. He left Vichy and traveled around the French Riviera. He
hoped he could rest and relax for a while.

Varian knew that his time in France was coming to an end. He
also knew that his stay there had caused a strain in his marriage.
Eileen had suffered from his extended absence. It may be that she
even considered their marriage over, because in a letter to her on August 5, Varian wrote:

The weather is very bad, and I am depressed. I am taking a vacation,
and not enjoying it. I wish I could leave for home right away, but I feel
I must stay until my successor arrives if I possibly can. Your last letter
still weighs very heavily on my mind and depresses me very much . . .

Please give me a couple of weeks more before you make up your
mind to leave me. Then I'll be back to try to straighten things out.

For about two weeks, Varian traveled alone to Sanary, Saint-
Tropez, Cannes, Nice, and Monte Carlo. He kept in touch with the

ARC office by telephone, and occasionally members of his staff traveled to meet him wherever he was.

Varian usually enjoyed the incredible views of blue sky, picture-perfect beaches, and quaint towns on the coast of France. But on this trip he was sick with sinus problems and overwhelmed by the turmoil at work and at home. He wrote Eileen from Cannes on August 17: "As for my holiday, it is exhausting me completely. I know of nothing more tiring than resting, and I was already worn out before I began."

Twelve days past the deadline for leaving that de Rodellec du Porzic had given him, Varian went back to Marseilles. He'd stayed away so long that the dates on his passport and visas had expired. Varian hoped de Rodellec du Porzic had been bluffing about making him leave.

Varian walked back into the ARC office on Wednesday, August 27. It didn't take long for him to find out that the chief of police had not been bluffing. On Friday two police detectives arrived with an order to take Varian into custody. It was signed by de Rodellec du Porzic. The Vichy police were actually going to kick him out of France.

Varian spent the next twenty-six hours locked up. He slept on a table. He was informed that he would be taken to the Spanish border and forced out of France. When Varian explained that all his paperwork had expired, they assured him that it would be completed at the border. Inspector Garandel, a Vichy policeman, had been given the job of seeing that Varian left France.

"It is my duty to show you that we French are not barbarians," explained Inspector Garandel after shaking hands with Varian. Garandel treated Varian with respect and seemed embarrassed by the task he'd been assigned.

Inspector Garandel escorting Varian out of France.

Police detectives took Varian to the ARC office. It would be his last visit there. Danny had left for Vichy to see if he could stop Varian's expulsion. Most of the office staff had gone for the day. Varian emptied the contents of his desk drawer into a cardboard box.

Next the detectives drove Varian to the Villa Air-Bel. They gave him one hour to collect his belongings, which included Clovis, his black poodle. From there they took him to the Gare Saint-Charles. It was then after six in the evening. Just as he had on the day he'd arrived, Varian walked to the top of the massive marble staircase and gazed out over Marseilles. The city where he had lived for nearly thirteen months was quiet. He took one last look at the mountains in the distance and at the Notre-Dame de la Garde Basilica, still standing guard over the city.

He turned away and walked into the train station with Inspector Garandel.

By this time most of Varian's team had heard what was happening, and nine members had gathered at the station. They came prepared to travel all the way to the border with him.

Together, they all traveled by train to the border town of Cerbère. Just as Varian expected, when the border police saw that his papers were outdated, they refused to let him cross the border. Inspector Garandel explained the situation, but the policeman would not make an exception.

Garandel telephoned his boss. The American Embassy would need to reissue Varian's travel documents. Inspector Garandel was ordered to lock Varian in the local jail until the documents arrived. Nevertheless, Garandel assured Varian that he would stay in a hotel, not the jail.

For the five days that it took for Varian's papers to arrive, Danny and some of the rest of Varian's staff stayed with him in Cerbère. Inspector Garandel didn't act like a policeman guarding a prisoner. He behaved more like a supervisor whose job was to make sure Varian got across the border. Each day Garandel visited acquaintances in the area and left Varian and his friends alone.

It gave them plenty of time to discuss the future of the ARC. From that point on, it would be led by Danny Bénédite, a Frenchman. An American replacement for Varian would never arrive.

Rain poured from the sky on September 6, 1941, the day Varian left France. The gray, dreary weather matched their mood as Varian and his staff ate their last lunch together. Around the table, long moments of silence took the place of their usual mealtime chatter. None of them knew what hardships lay ahead. None knew what the outcome of World War II would be. Would Hitler ultimately be victorious and take over all of Europe and the rest of the world? Would they ever see each other again? Would the Vichy police or the Gestapo come for them in the middle of the night? Would they have enough food to survive the winter?

Finally the moment that they'd all been dreading came. Inspector Garandel would accompany Varian across the Spanish border into Portbou, and see that Varian boarded the train to Barcelona before he returned to France.

The conductor called out for the passengers to board. One by one, Varian's team hugged and kissed him goodbye.

Varian took this photo of the staff members who accompanied him to the border right before he boarded the train that took him out of France. Left to right: Paul Schmierer, Helen Hessel, Danny Bénédite, Marcel Verzeano, Lucie Heymann, Jeanne Vialin, Charles Wolff (who would later be killed by the French police), Louis Coppermann, and Annette Pouppos.

Varian stepped aboard the train. He stood on the bottom step as the train pulled away. Varian looked at his friends, who were standing in a line on the platform. He took out his handkerchief and waved goodbye. His team waved back to him. They were still waving when the train entered the tunnel that separated France from Spain.

As his train moved through the Spanish countryside in the rain, Varian was filled with sadness. He already felt a deep sense of loss for France and the friends he had left there. They had bonded and worked together toward a common goal as a team. Varian knew he would not return to France for a long time—at least not until the war was over, and there was no way to know when that would be. His work in Marseilles had cost him a lot of time and energy, but it was worth it. Now his work was done. It was all over. The work of the American Relief Center would continue without him.

On September 7, while in Barcelona, Varian wrote to Eileen:

> What I do know is that I have lived far more intensely in this last year, far more objectively, actively, really, if you like, than I ever have before, and that the experience has changed me profoundly . . . I do not think I shall ever be quite the same person I was when I kissed you goodbye at the airport . . . For the experiences of ten, fifteen and even twenty years have been pressed into one . . .
>
> I have learned to live with people, and to work with them. I have developed, or discovered within me, powers of resourcefulness, of imagination and of courage which I never before knew I possessed. And I have fought a fight, against enormous odds, of which, in spite of the final defeat, I think I can always be proud . . .
>
> The knowledge of that fact has given me a new quality which I think I needed: self-confidence . . . I don't know whether you will like the change or not: I rather suspect you won't. But it is there, and it is there to stay . . .
>
> I just want to tell you that you are going to find your husband a changed man—and to put you on your guard against trying to change him back again to what he was before.

On September 14, in a letter to his mother, Varian wrote: "I knew before I left New York that I was going to be in for the hardest job I had ever undertaken in my life." Although the job had been demanding, Varian was proud that he had persevered and stayed as long as he had. He said, "I stayed because the refugees needed me. But it took courage, and courage is a quality I hadn't previously been sure I possessed."

Varian tried to explain how it felt to go from Nazi-controlled France, a country ravaged by war, to Portugal, one that was enjoying peace. "Coming out of France today is like coming up out of a dark cave toward the light. Literally and figuratively." In France there wasn't enough of anything, including food. Yet in Portugal, there was plenty of everything: real tea, cameras, typewriters, magazines, newspapers, and food. Varian wrote, "(. . . I have been going around Lisbon all afternoon, goggle-eyed, like a child at his first circus, unable to decide between popcorn and peanuts, bananas and ice cream, and finally taking them *all* . . .). But most of all, you get a feeling of *freedom*."

It took about six weeks for Varian to complete his travel arrangements back to America. During that time he worked at the office of the Unitarian Service Committee and attempted to improve the escape routes his refugees were using through Spain and Portugal. Throughout October the autumn weather in Lisbon turned his thoughts again and again to the leaves that skittered around the streets of Marseilles as the mistral blew in. It made him sad and homesick—not for America but for France.

Varian considered things he could have done differently and mistakes he'd made. He wrote Danny on October 20 that he should have spent more time cultivating friendships with both French and American officials. He felt that he and Danny were "rather lacking in social graces, rather shy, rather self-conscious in company . . . People outside of the office did not realise the real reason; many of them thought that we were snobbish or stand-offish (this is very often the case with shy people). The result was that some of them came to dislike or mistrust us—merely because they did not know us. This was unfortunate because when we needed them we could not count on them."

Varian had been away for nearly fifteen months by the time he reached New York, on November 2, 1941. As soon as he arrived, reporters asked him about his work in France. He publicly criticized American authorities. An article that ran in the November 3 edition of *The New York Times* said that Varian "accused the State Department of the United States of acting 'stupidly' " in regard to its visa policies. An article in the New York *Daily News* on the same day quoted Varian as saying, "Red tape, with which the State Department enshrouds refugee procedure, is also making it easier for the Gestapo to prevent the exodus of anti-Nazis from Hitler-occupied lands."

Varian Fry was home at last, but the transition was hard for him. He had changed a lot. Eileen had changed, too. The long separation had put a lot of stress on their relationship, and their marriage was in trouble. The next year they divorced, although they remained good friends.

For more than a year Varian had dealt with matters of life and death all day, every day. His every thought had been about the safety of his protégés. Now it was all out of his control. He missed the danger, excitement, and challenge of the work. He missed his coworkers, who had become his friends. He missed France. The loss left him feeling empty.

On November 10, 1941, Varian wrote to John Graham, a friend in Lisbon:

New York depresses me very much. It has been an extraordinary experience to come here from Lisbon overnight—from a continent at

war to a continent at peace—and to find that my countrymen are only
just beginning to wake up to the menace that hangs over all of us . . .

New York depresses me for another reason. It is noisy and dirty
and full of meaningless activity.

Varian hoped to work at the Emergency Rescue Committee office. However, repeated clashes between Varian and the ERC leaders over Jay Allen and many other things left hard feelings between them. Varian had grown accustomed to being the boss, and felt that he knew best what needed to be done to help his team in Marseilles. He wrote Danny on November 25 that the workings of the office left "much to be desired, and it is going to be a long uphill job to improve them. I have little or no authority here, and must proceed patiently and tactfully." The strained relationship worsened as Varian tried to tell the people at the ERC office what to do and how to do it. They had been doing their jobs without Varian's input, and they didn't appreciate his interference.

Only a little more than a month after Varian returned, America would no longer be a nation at peace. On December 7, 1941, the nation of Japan attacked U.S. Navy ships at Pearl Harbor in Hawaii. America entered World War II, a war that would rage all over the globe. Nations led by Germany, Italy, and Japan became known as the Axis nations. Those led by the United States, Britain, the Soviet Union, and China became known as the Allies.

America's entering the war brought changes to the Emergency Rescue Committee. In the early days of 1942 the ERC joined forces with the International Relief Association to form a new organization that would be known as the International Rescue and Relief Committee. This name would later be shortened to the International Rescue Committee (IRC), which still exists today. The merger meant that the Emergency Rescue Committee, which Varian had helped to create, no longer existed. Varian was not happy about the merger.

Finally, on February 13, 1942, Frank Kingdon, the president of the Emergency Rescue Committee, by then known as the International Rescue and Relief Committee, fired Varian.

Varian continued to exchange letters with Danny, who was running the American Relief Center in Marseilles. But then, on June 2, 1942, Vichy police closed it down.

It is impossible to know exactly how many people Varian Fry helped out of France. It was too dangerous to keep incriminating records, knowing the Vichy police could have searched for them at any time. However, Varian knew he'd made arrangements for two hundred British soldiers to cross into Spain. He also knew that he had arranged the escape of at least seven hundred refugees—and most of these seven hundred had a spouse and children. Then, after Varian left Marseilles, the ARC succeeded in getting out another three hundred refugees and their families. A conservative estimate is that Varian and his team arranged for more than two thousand people to leave France safely.

In 1942 Varian began writing a book, *Surrender on Demand*, about his experiences in Marseilles. He knew the story could not be told until the war was over and his friends in France were no longer in danger of being arrested by the Vichy police or the Gestapo. Varian wrote a foreword for the book that revealed how deeply his experiences in Marseilles had affected him:

I have tried—God knows I have tried—to get back again into the mood of American life since I left France for the last time. But it doesn't work. There is only one way left to try, and that is the way I am going to try now. If I can get it all out, put it all down just as it happened, if I can make others see it and feel it as I did, then maybe I can sleep soundly again at night, the way I used to before I took the Clipper to Lisbon. Maybe I can become a normal human being again, exorcize the ghosts which haunt me, stop living in another world, come back to the world of America. But I do know that I can't do that until I have told the story—all of it.

When the book was published three years later, this original, heartfelt foreword was not included.

Like many heroes before him and after, Varian found out that his fight for the freedom of others came at a high price—his peace of mind. But he had willingly gone to help the refugees in France. He would make the same choice all over again.

As he worked on the book, Varian tried to join the United States military. He was rejected because he had developed stomach ulcers. Next he applied for various government jobs to support the war effort, including one at the Office of Facts and Figures. Finally he got a job as an editor at a magazine called *The New Republic*.

[Aftermath]

EVEN BACK IN AMERICA, VARIAN DID WHAT HE COULD
to help the refugees in France. He used his talents as a writer and
speaker to educate people about what the Nazis were doing to the
Jews of Europe. On December 21, 1942, the magazine where he
worked, *The New Republic*, ran an article Varian wrote entitled "The
Massacre of the Jews." In it Varian called for the people and churches
all over the world to make the atrocities against the Jews known. He
also called on the United States to open its doors to more refugees.
Varian warned the world that Jews were being starved to death,
worked to death, and packed into cattle cars and shipped to eastern
Europe to be killed. He wrote: "According to a report to the President by leaders of American Jewish groups, nearly 2,000,000 European Jews have already been slain since the war began, and the
remaining 5,000,000 now living under Nazi control are scheduled to
be destroyed."

Also in the article, Varian told about a letter he had seen from
a Jew in Poland. Written in German, it was allowed to pass the
censor in Germany because the writer used Hebrew words, which the

Jewish people in Auschwitz. In May of 1944, when these women and children arrived, they didn't understand that the Nazi in charge had just "selected" them to go to their deaths in the gas chambers.

censor did not understand, as if they were names. Varian quoted the letter:

> I spoke to Mr. Jaeger . . . ["Mr. Jaeger" means the Germans.] He told me that he will invite all relatives of the family Achenu [Hebrew for "our brethren," i. e., the Jews], with the exception of Miss Eisenzweig [probably means those working in the iron mines], from Warsaw to his mansion "Kewer" [Hebrew for "tomb"]. Uncle Gerusch [Hebrew for "deportation"] also works in Warsaw; he is a very capable worker. My friend Miso [Hebrew for "death"] now works with him. I am alone here; I feel very lonely . . . Please pray for me. [Bracketed passages in original.]

Varian tried to get Americans to understand that each and every Jew in Europe was in danger. But even with proof that the Holocaust

Nazi leaders being questioned about their war crimes at the Nuremberg Trials. The defendants, left to right, beginning in the front row: Hermann Göring, Rudolf Hess, Joachim von Ribbentrop, Wilhelm Keitel, Ernst Kaltenbrunner, Alfred Rosenberg, Hans Frank, Wilhelm Frick, Julius Streicher, Walther Funk, Hjalmar Schacht. Back row, from left to right: Karl Dönitz, Erich Raeder, Baldur von Schirach, Fritz Sauckel, Alfred Jodl, Franz von Papen, Arthur Seyss-Inquart, Albert Speer, Konstantin von Neurath, and Hans Fritzsche.

was taking place, America and other countries took in too few Jewish refugees. As World War II continued, just as Varian feared, some concentration camps turned into extermination camps where Jews were ruthlessly and systematically murdered.

After years of great sacrifice and loss of life all over the world, the Allies won the war in 1945. The Nazis had been defeated and Hitler had committed suicide in Berlin. At war's end, it is estimated that the Nazis had murdered more than 6,000,000 Jews, 1,500,000 of them children, and 5,000,000 non-Jews.

The Allies put the surviving leaders of Hitler's Third Reich—the

Third Empire, as the Nazis named their regime—on trial for their war crimes. The trial was held in Nuremberg, Germany, the same city where the anti-Semitic Nuremberg Laws had been announced in 1935. Of the twenty-four major war criminals accused, twelve men were sentenced to hang; three were sentenced to life in prison; four were sent to prison for years; three were set free; one committed suicide while being held; and one was unable to stand trial because of his physical and mental condition.

When the war was over, Varian felt he could finally share the story of his work in Marseilles. His co-workers would no longer be in danger when the truth was told. *Surrender on Demand* was published in 1945.

Varian was relieved to find out that Beamish, Danny, Jean, Maurice, Charlie, Gussie, and Hans and Lisa Fittko all survived the war. Now all of them would have to find a way to deal with their wartime experiences and make a new life. In a letter to Jean on January 9, 1945, Varian wrote that he had been undergoing psychoanalysis and that it was "quite a hard job." He told Jean he was living alone with his two dogs, Clovis and Clovis's "wife," his books, and his pictures.

Jean wrote back: "You describe your life as a peaceful and occupied one, rather lonely perhaps, but surrounded with books, dogs and pictures . . . From the sound of your letter, I gather you do not feel very happy, although you would like to pretend to be."

By 1946 Varian decided to set aside his work as a writer and editor and go into business. He bought a production studio that made commercials and educational films, but ultimately it ended in bankruptcy. After this he worked as a freelance writer for several big companies, including Coca-Cola. He remained interested in social causes and was on the board of directors for the American Civil Liberties Union and the International League for the Rights of Man.

Varian, always the rescuer, nursed this injured robin back to health.

In 1948, six years after they divorced, Eileen was diagnosed with cancer. Varian sat by the hospital bedside of his dear friend each day and read to her. Eileen Fry died on May 12, 1948.

On November 11, 1950, Varian married a beautiful young woman named Annette Riley, who was sixteen years younger than he. Together they had three children, Thomas, Sylvia, and James. Varian and his family moved to a large home in Ridgefield, Connecticut, where Varian could enjoy his family, watching birds, and gardening.

As the years went by, the two different sides of Varian's personality became more noticeable. He could be a charming, funny story-teller, but he could also be moody, argumentative, and bossy. Varian and Annette's marriage was difficult for this reason.

In the early 1960s Varian decided he wanted to return to his favorite subjects, Latin and Greek. He got a job teaching high school in Connecticut. But after a disagreement with the Coca-Cola Company, Varian lost his freelance job writing materials for them. Without the extra income, his family had to move to a smaller home.

More than twenty years had come and gone since Varian and the International Rescue Committee (IRC) had parted ways. In 1963, however, the IRC wanted to publicly honor Varian for his work in Marseilles for the cause of freedom. It was the first recognition Varian received. One of his favorite protégés, Jacques Lipchitz, pre-

Jacques Lipchitz presenting the medal of the International Rescue Committee to Varian in recognition of his work in Marseilles.

sented Varian with a medal. Lipchitz had become a world-famous artist since he moved to America. His sculptures were displayed in art museums all over the world. Jacques Lipchitz always gave Varian the credit he deserved for what he had done in Marseilles.

Later in 1963 Varian came up with a fundraising idea for the IRC. He would ask some of the famous modern artists he had helped get out of France to create a painting. Each artist would create a litho-graph, a type of print, that would remind people of the many refugees who had fled the Nazis. Each piece of art would be as indi-vidual as the artist who created it. The plan was that after all the artists finished, the International Rescue Committee would compile their pieces into a set that would be titled *Flight*. When the sets were sold to the public, Varian would get 10 percent of the sales as pay-ment for making all the contacts and arrangements.

Varian was excited about working on this project, probably more excited than he'd been in a long time. Since many of the artists had returned to France after the war was over, Varian would get the chance to revisit his beloved Marseilles.

In the fall of 1964 Varian once again saw Marseilles. War damage, such as the destruction of much of the Old Port, had long since been repaired. Varian was thrilled to be back. On a postcard to his wife, Annette, Varian wrote: "I can hardly believe I am really in Marseille again: I think I had given up, long ago, the hope of ever seeing it again. It has changed much since I first arrived here, more than 24 years ago . . . But much has not changed at all, and I find myself growing very sentimental."

Unfortunately, Varian found the lithograph project more frustrating and difficult to accomplish than he'd imagined. And once again, his trip to France lasted longer than he'd expected, more than five months. Getting busy artists to agree to create a piece of art for charity took time. Some refugees whom Varian had helped get out of France happily contributed a piece of art. But other artists would not participate. Varian asked André Breton to write an introduction to the art portfolio. Breton, his wife, and daughter had lived at the Villa Air-Bel with Varian and the others. Months went by before Varian got an answer, and not from Breton directly. The message came in the form of a memo from a mutual acquaintance to Charles Sternberg, director of the International Rescue Committee. The memo relayed Breton's position on the issue. It said:

> The whole matter is a "malentendu" [misunderstanding], never did he [Breton] think or promise to write anything about Marseille. This is not within the range of things he does.
>
> He says he had given to Varian Fry one of his books with a nice and friendly dedication, but that's all and no more is to be expected.

Ultimately, twelve different artists contributed a piece for the *Flight* portfolio. Only four of the contributors, Jacques Lipchitz, Marc Chagall, André Masson, and Wifredo Lam had been Varian's protégés in Marseilles. The other eight were Eugene Berman, Alexander Calder, Adolph Gottlieb, Joan Miró, Robert Motherwell, Edouard Pignon, Maria Elena Vieira da Silva, and Fritz Wotruba.

The lithograph that Jacques Lipchitz donated, at Varian's request, to the *Flight* portfolio for the International Rescue Committee.

Through the years, Varian had developed a tendency to be overly concerned about his health and, according to Sheila Isenberg's book, took too much medication. But now Varian truly wasn't well. While he was in France, he had a heart attack. Then, in letters home, he complained about continuing pain in his shoulders.

During Varian's trip to Europe, he wrote in a letter: "A number of my friends, French and other, here in Paris and elsewhere in France, have asked me why I don't wear 'the little ribbon' [the Legion of Honor Medal awarded to those who gave extraordinary service to France], and I have had to answer that I don't wear it because I have never been given the right to wear it." He added that "They have usually then said that I certainly ought to be given that right, because I did, in fact, much more for France than many étrangers [foreigners] who have received the decoration . . . One friend has even gotten a member of the Chamber of Deputies, Tomasini, to agree to present my name for some sort of decoration or other."

After he returned home, Varian continued to work on the *Flight* portfolio for the next several years.

At last, in 1967, Varian got some official recognition from France. For his work in Marseilles, the nation of France awarded Varian Fry the Cross of Chevalier of the Legion of Honor. Established by Em-

Varian Fry after receiving the Cross of Chevalier of the Legion of Honor, in 1967. The medal, shown here pinned to Varian's left lapel, was presented by Edouard Morot-Sir, the cultural counselor at the French Consulate. It was a proud moment for Varian, his wife, Annette, and their children, James, Sylvia, and Thomas.

peror Napoleon I, the Legion of Honor is the highest honor given in France. On April 12, 1967, the ceremony was held at the French Consulate in New York City.

That summer, Varian started writing a version of his story for young readers entitled *Assignment: Rescue, An Autobiography*. But he had trouble working. He was experiencing headaches and dizziness, and he checked into the hospital, but the doctors found nothing amiss.

While he was there, his mood swings worsened. Varian had been distant and difficult all summer, and now he asked Annette for a divorce. She arranged to get a quick divorce in Mexico. But on her return, she found Varian sad. When he was released from the hospital, he went back home with Annette.

In the fall, Varian began a new teaching job at a high school in Connecticut. He taught class on Thursday and Friday, the first two days of school, then went to spend the weekend with Annette and their children. At the beginning of the next week, Varian returned to the home he rented near the school.

On September 13, 1967, Varian went to bed, taking with him some research material for the new book project, *Assignment: Rescue*. Varian died that night from a cerebral hemorrhage, with memories of Marseilles scattered about him.

[Remembered]

EVERYTHING IN VARIAN'S LIFE BEFORE MARSEILLES
seemed to prepare him for the work he did there. Everything in Varian's life after Marseilles seemed to stand in the shadow of it. But for thirteen months in France, it all came together for Varian Fry. It was the perfect mix of the job, the challenge, and the man.

While most people chose to ignore what was happening to the Jews in Europe, Varian chose to do something about it. He went to Marseilles when others would not go. He stayed in Marseilles when others would not stay. He defied Hitler's plan to annihilate every Jew by arranging for the escape of many.

The nation of Israel acknowledged Varian's achievement by giving him its highest honor at Yad Vashem, the Holocaust Memorial in Jerusalem. In 1996 Varian Fry was named "Righteous Among the Nations," an accolade given to non-Jews who helped Jews during the Holocaust. He was the first American to receive this recognition.

Because of Varian, the lives of more than two thousand people did not end in concentration camps. Because of Varian, society would benefit from many of his protégés as they created art, music, photographs, movies, scientific theories, and books of fiction, history, and poetry. Because of Varian, these men and women could raise their children in a world without Hitler or his Gestapo.

Varian Fry knew it was impossible to rescue every Jew in Europe. But he knew it was possible to rescue some.

And he did.

APPENDIX

Danny Bénédite

Danny Bénédite took Varian Fry's place as the leader of the American Relief Center in Marseilles. After the center was shut down by the Gestapo, Danny began working with the French Resistance. Near the end of the war, he was captured and sentenced to death by firing squad, and escaped only when American troops landed. After the war, Danny and Theo divorced. He worked for various newspapers. Danny died in 1990.

Miriam Davenport Ebel

After Miriam Davenport left Marseilles, she traveled to Yugoslavia, where she married her fiancé. They reached America safely; however, their marriage ended in divorce. Miriam then married William Burke, a professor at Princeton University. While living there, she worked for Albert Einstein at the Emergency Committee of Atomic Scientists. After she and her second husband moved to Iowa, she worked as a painter and sculptor. Burke died, and eventually Miriam was married again, this time to Charles Ebel. She returned to school and in 1973 earned a Ph.D. Miriam died of cancer on September 13, 1999.

Charlie Fawcett

When Charlie Fawcett left Marseilles, his plan was to get to Britain to join the Royal Air Force. But before he could get there, he was arrested and questioned by the Gestapo. Charlie escaped and made it to Britain. However, he was sick with tuberculosis and was unable to join the war effort. By the time he arrived back in America, Charlie was seriously ill. He was hospitalized for an extended period of time, but eventually recovered. Charlie continued his life of adventure and became an actor and director of movies made all over the world. He lives in London.

Lisa and Hans Fittko

Lisa and Hans Fittko escaped Europe at the end of 1941 and went to Cuba. In 1948, they moved to Chicago, Illinois. Hans died in 1960 and was later honored by Yad Vashem as "Righteous Among the Nations" (Lisa was Jewish; Hans was not). More than forty years after the events of World War II, Lisa wrote about her experiences in *Escape through the Pyrenees* and *Solidarity and Treason: Resistance and Exile, 1933–40*. Lisa was honored in 1986 with the Distinguished Service Medal, First Class, of the Federal Republic of Germany. She died of pneumonia on March 12, 2005, at the age of ninety-five.

Bill Freier (Wilhelm Spira) and Mina

Bill Freier was betrayed and arrested for forging documents. Before being sent to Auschwitz, he was allowed to marry Mina. Bill survived the concentration camp. After the camp was liberated, he was reunited with his wife, who had given birth in his absence to their son, François. Sadly, the stress of war caused Mina to have a nervous breakdown. She was placed in an asylum, where she died in 1951.

Jean Gemähling

Jean Gemähling also worked with the French Resistance after the American Relief Center closed its doors. He was betrayed, arrested, and imprisoned in Marseilles, but escaped. When free, he returned to work with the Resistance and continued throughout the war. He died on May 2, 2003.

Mary Jayne Gold

After the war, Mary Jayne Gold returned to live on the Riviera in southern France. She never married or had children. She died of pancreatic cancer on October 5, 1997, in her villa near Saint-Tropez. She was eighty-eight.

Ernst Hanfstaengl

After meeting with Varian Fry in 1935, German-American Ernst Hanfstaengl continued working for Hitler and the Nazi Party. But by 1937 Hanfstaengl had fallen out of favor with Adolf Hitler and had to run for his life. He escaped to Switzerland and eventually made his way to England, where he was placed in an internment camp. When the United States entered the war, Hanfstaengl was brought to Washington, D.C., to monitor German radio broadcasts and send analyses of what he heard to the White House. In 1944, he was returned to the British and put in an internment camp in Germany. After the war, Hanfstaengl made his home in Munich, Germany. He died on November 6, 1975.

Albert O. Hirschman (Beamish)

Albert O. Hirschman (Beamish), who already had a Ph.D. when he worked with Varian Fry in Marseilles, arrived in the United States in 1941. He went to the University of California at Berkeley for a research fellowship and later joined the American Army. After World War II, Dr. Hirschman became one of the world's leading experts on economics. He authored books and taught at Columbia University,

Yale University, Harvard University, and Princeton University, where he is now professor emeritus.

Justus Rosenberg (Gussie)

In September of 1941, Gussie tried to cross the Pyrenees to make it on his own through Spain to Portugal, but he was arrested by the French border police and thrown into jail. When he came up for trial, the sympathetic judge fined him only for having traveled into a guarded zone without a permit and set him free. Through contacts Gussie had made while a courier at the ARC, he joined the French Resistance and was assigned to its intelligence section, then to a guerrilla group operating in the Rhone Valley, and on the landing of the American forces, to their 630 Tank Destroyer Battalion as a reconnaissance guide and interpreter. When the war ended, Gussie returned to Paris to complete his studies. In 1946 he came with a preferential visa to the United States, where he earned a Ph.D. and academic appointments at various institutions of higher learning. Since 1962 he has been a professor of comparative literature at Bard College and The New School for Social Research.

Marcel Verzeano (Maurice)

When Verzeano arrived in the United States, he became an intern and then a resident at hospitals in New York City. From 1943 to 1946 he was a member of the United States Army Medical Corps. During his time in the army, he rose to the rank of captain and was awarded two medals. He was made a Knight of the Crown of Italy in 1945. Later he worked at UCLA doing research on brain waves. He died in 2006.

SOURCE NOTES

To simplify the notes, the following abbreviations are used:

AH Archives of the Holocaust. Karen J. Greenberg, ed. Columbia University Library, Varian Fry Papers. *Archives of the Holocaust: An International Collection of Selected Documents*, vol. 5 (New York: Garland Publishing, 1990).

AR Varian Fry, *Assignment: Rescue, An Autobiography* (New York: Scholastic in conjunction with the United States Holocaust Memorial Museum, 1968).

AUE Miriam Davenport Ebel, *An Unsentimental Education: A Memoir*. Posted at www.varianfry.org with the permission of Dr. Charles Ebel. www.varianfry.org/ebel_en.htm (1999).

CM Mary Jayne Gold, *Crossroads Marseilles 1940* (Garden City, New York, N.Y.: Doubleday, 1980).

EF Eileen Fry

ERC Emergency Rescue Committee

ETP Lisa Fittko, *Escape Through the Pyrenees*; trans. David Koblick (Evanston, Ill.: Northwestern University Press, 2000).

SD Varian Fry, *Surrender on Demand* (Boulder, Colo.: Johnson Books in conjunction with the United States Holocaust Memorial Museum, 1997).

TFM   Hans Sahl, *The Few and the Many*; trans. Richard and Clara Winston (New York: Harcourt, Brace and World, 1962).

VF   Varian Fry

VFP   Varian Fry Papers, Rare Book and Manuscript Library, Columbia University

[Witness]

3   "When Jewish blood": Varian Fry, "The Massacre of the Jews," *The New Republic*, December 21, 1942, 816–18.

4   "Jew"; "The best Jew": "Editor Describes Rioting in Berlin," *The New York Times*, July 17, 1935.

4   "This is a holiday": "Eyewitness Story of Berlin Horror," ibid. and *New York Post*, July 16, 1935.

12   "The French Government is obliged": *SD*, xii.

[Preparation]

14   "The President has seen": letter from Eleanor Roosevelt to VF, July 8, 1940, VFP, Box 1, 2015.

16   "I'm not right for the job"; "I felt a deep love"; "You're it": *AR*, 3, 5, 4.

18   "the Committee realizes"; "to attempt to locate": letter from ERC to VF, August 3, 1940, AH, document 1.

20   "This Goop bounces on the bed": Arthur Fry, father of Varian Fry. VFP, Box 11 2000–2066.

24   In it he recalled that Varian felt: Lincoln Kirstein, *Mosaic: Memoirs* (New York: Farrar, Straus and Giroux, 1994), 101.

24   But at other times, according to a biography: Sheila Isenberg, *A Hero of Our Own: The Story of Varian Fry* (New York: Random House, 2001), 57.

26   "When Jewish blood": Varian Fry, "The Massacre of the Jews," *The New Republic*, December 21, 1942, 816–18.

[Papers]

31   "Aha, an American"; *AR*, 7.

32, 34   "drains and garlic"; "bewildered": *SD*, 3, 4.

34   "the admission we sought": Hertha Pauli, *Break of Time* (New York: Hawthorn Books, 1972), 167–68.

35, 36   "What do you mean"; "half-filled sack of flour"; "You must save us": *SD*, 5, 6, 6.

36   "Mr. Fry did the job": Alma Mahler Werfel, *And the Bridge Is Love* (New York: Harcourt, Brace, 1958), 265.

39   "Do exactly as you are told": Lion Feuchtwanger, *The Devil in France*; trans. Elisabeth Abbott (New York: Viking, 1941), 260.

40   "Mother seeks baby"; "Generous reward for information": *SD*, 20, 20.

[Choices]

44   "When I appeared at the hotel": *TFM*, 306.

48   "a full-blown American 'preppie' ": *AUE*.

48, 51   "The Book of Ruth was read"; "Although I am terrible at faces": Miriam Davenport Ebel. Quoted from *And Crown Thy Good: Varian Fry in Marseilles*, forthcoming documentary by Pierre Sauvage, Varian Fry Institute / Chambon Foundation production.

52   "You must not go too far": *AR*, 31.

53   "In the beginning, I was an amateur": Miriam Davenport Ebel. Quoted from *And Crown Thy Good: Varian Fry in Marseilles*, forthcoming documentary by Pierre Sauvage, Varian Fry Institute / Chambon Foundation production.

53, 54   "impossible decisions"; "We had no way of knowing": *SD*, 30, 31.

54   "the pleasure of being able to help even a few people": letter from VF to EF, September 7, 1940, VFP, Box 3, 2017.

54   "With us and with our clients he was warm": *AUE*.

57   "It's the police": *SD*, 33.

59   "Well, I can see nothing wrong": *AR*, 21–22.

[Plans]

63   "Heil Hitler"; "Well, it looks like the Gestapo": *AR*, 33, 33.

66   "I'll see you soon in New York": *SD*, 17.

71   "might even do some interviewing"; "sounded frivolous and he assured Miriam": *CM*, 153, 159–60.

73   "rough diamond": *SD*, 53.

[Escape]

75, 80, 82 "If you will come with me"; "'Well,' I said, measuring my words"; "We are obliged to act": *SD*, 57, 64, 65.

84   "steep, stony trail that soon vanished": Alma Mahler Werfel, *And the Bridge Is Love* (New York: Harcourt, Brace, 1958), 166.

84, 85 "When the *gardes mobiles*"; "So you are the son": *SD*, 68, 69.

[Spy]

86, 89, 91 "it would be all right"; "I am willing to place $10,000"; "activities of Dr. Bohn and Mr. Fry"; "This government cannot countenance": *SD*, 70, 77, 80, 81.

92   "RETURNING SOON AS SUCCESSOR ARRIVES": cable from VF to EF, September 25, 1940, VFP, Box 3, 2017.

92   "OFFICE HERE WOULD COLLAPSE": cable from VF to EF, October 1, 1940, VFP, Box 3, 2017.

93   "I hope you realize": letter from EF to VF, October 19, 1940, VFP, Box 3, 2017.

94   "Sure, we know all about Fry": *SD*, 93.

97   "*Combien?*' he asked": *ETP*, 119.

[Undercover]

106 "The *maddening* thing"; "After all, I can't stay forever"; "I still see dozens of people": letter from VF to EF, October 27, 1940, VFP, Box 3, 2017.

106 "Almost from the moment": letter from VF to Lilian Fry, November 3, 1940, VFP, Box 3, 2017.

107 "A shady avenue led us up a gentle slope": *CM*, 240.

110 "If you ever feel inclined": letter from EF to VF, November 10, 1940, VFP, Box 3, 2017.

112 "RETURNING SOONAS SUCCESSOR ARRIVES": cable from VF to EF, November 16, 1940, VFP, Box 3, 2017.

112 "What is wrong with our concentration camps?"; "How many times do we have to tell you": *SD*, 127, 129.

114 "This job is like death": letter from VF to EF, November 29, 1940, VFP, Box 3, 2017.

115 "I may still with luck": letter from VF to Lilian Fry, November 3, 1940, VFP, Box 3, 2017.

[Enemies]

117, 118, 119 "I just have to get a handkerchief"; "Engage that guy in conversation"; "got tired of learning"; "With Beamish and Beamish alone I could be perfectly candid": *SD*, 137, 137, 150, 151.

121 "Very little is now being done": "Lisbon's Refugees Now Put at 8,000" by James B. Reston, *The New York Times*, December 15, 1940.

122 "By a decree issued in Strasbourg": "Property of Jews in Alsace Is Confiscated; Finer Furnishings Sent to Reich by Trainload," by Telephone to *The New York Times*, December 17, 1940.

125 "I assume that you are making preparations": letter from Jay Allen to VF, January 2, 1941, VFP, Box 2, 2015.

125 "I don't know what to do"; "I wonder whether": letter from VF to EF, January 5, 1941, VFP, Box 3, 2017.

126, 127   "not had time—or apparently, interest"; "an organization which is known all over"; "not once asked what the weekly budget"; "this office is not your office": letter from VF to ERC, January 21, 1941, AH, Document 13.

128   "I've never had a job": letter from VF to Lilian Fry, February 3, 1941, VFP, Box 3, 2017.

128   "this afternoon Mr. J. A. made his first": letter from VF to EF, February 15, 1941, AH, Document 15.

[Betrayed]

129   "Naturally I was kinda pleased": letter from VF to EF, April 21, 1941, VFP, Box 3, 2017.

131   "We are all hungry here all the time": letter from VF to EF, March 18, 1941, VFP, Box 3, 2017.

131   "beefsteaks, mashed potatoes with butter": letter from VF to Arthur Fry, May 14, 1941, VFP, Box 3, 2017.

133   "In my suitcase were a great many little slips": *TFM*, 307.

135   "If he isn't out in half an hour": *SD*, 207.

135   cut Varian's salary: cable from ERC in New York to VF, February 2, 1941, VFP, AH, Document 14.

136   "Much love if you're interested": letter from EF to VF, February 18, 1941, VFP, Box 3, 2017.

136   "Miss you badly": letter from EF to VF, March 17, 1941, VFP, Box 3, 2017.

136   "The anti-semitism of France": letter from VF to EF, May 3, 1941, VFP, Box 3, 2017.

137, 138, 139   "was less than five feet tall"; "I don't like the look of things"; "Twice a day, on my way"; "I felt like an awful fool": *SD*, 47, 211, 213, 214.

140   "arrests, searches of the house and the office": letter from VF to Lilian Fry, September 14, 1941, VFP, AH, Document 18.

140   "My instructions are to renew it only": *SD*, 219.

140 "there is nothing I can do for your husband": letter from Eleanor Roosevelt to EF, May 13, 1941, VFP, Box 1, 2015.

[Expelled]

141, 142 "I hope you are not going to come back"; "Please don't wait six weeks": letter from EF to VF, July 8, 1941, VFP, Box 3, 2017.

142 "You have caused my good friend the Consul-General": *SD*, 222–24.

145 "Remember that . . . I have been working": letter from VF to EF, July 31, 1941, VFP, Box 3, 2017.

145 "The weather is very bad": letter VF to EF, August 5, 1941, VFP, Box 3, 2017.

146 "As for my holiday, it is exhausting me completely": letter from VF to EF, August 17, 1941, VFP, Box 3, 2017.

146 "It is my duty to show you": *SD*, 227.

150 "What I do know is that I have lived": letter from VF to EF, September 7, 1941, VFP, Box 3, 2017.

150, 151 "I knew before I left New York"; "I stayed because the refugees"; "Coming out of France today", "(. . . I have been going around Lisbon": letter from VF to Lilian Fry, September 14, 1941, VFP, Box 3, 2017.

151 "rather lacking in social graces": letter from VF to Danny Bénédite, October 20, 1941, VFP, AH, Document 21.

152 "accused the State Department": *The New York Times*, November 3, 1941.

152 "Red tape, with which the State Department": "Blames U.S. Delays for Refugee Perils," *Daily News*, November 3, 1941.

152 "New York depresses me very much": letter from VF to John Graham, November 10, 1941, VFP, Box 6, 2021.

153 "much to be desired": letter from VF to Danny Bénédite, November 25, 1941, VFP, Box 2, 2015.

154 "I have tried—God knows I have tried": *SD*, 241.

[Aftermath]

156, 157 "According to a report to the President"; "I spoke to Mr. Jaegar": Varian Fry, "The Massacre of the Jews," *The New Republic*, December 1942, 816, 817.

159 "quite a hard job": letter from VF to Jean Gemähling, January 9, 1945, VFP, Box 4, 2018.

159 "You describe your life": letter from Jean Gemähling to VF, March 21, 1945, VFP, AH, Document 35.

161 "I can hardly believe I am really in Marseille again": postcard from VF to Annette Fry, November 19, 1964, VFP, Box of photos, #9749.

162 "The whole matter is a 'malentendu' ": memo from Hanne Benzion to Charles Sternberg, January 31, 1966, VFP, Box 3, 2017.

163 took too much medication: Sheila Isenberg, *A Hero of Our Own: The Story of Varian Fry* (New York: Random House, 2001), 265.

163 "A number of my friends": letter from VF to Stéphane Hessel, February 21, 1965, VFP, AH, Document 45.

164 He was experiencing headaches and dizziness: Sheila Isenberg, *A Hero of Our Own: The Story of Varian Fry* (New York: Random House, 2001), 267.

BIBLIOGRAPHY

[Books]

Barron, Stephanie. *Exiles + Emigrés: The Flight of European Artists from Hitler.* New York: Harry N. Abrams in conjunction with the Los Angeles County Museum of Art, 1997.

Dawson, Mark. *Flight: Refugees and the Quest for Freedom—The History of the International Rescue Committee 1933–1993.* New York: International Rescue Committee, 1993.

Epstein, Helen. *Children of the Holocaust: Conversations with Sons and Daughters of Survivors.* New York: Putnam's, 1979.

Feuchtwanger, Lion. *The Devil in France: My Encounter With Him in the Summer of 1940.* Trans. Elisabeth Abbott. New York: Viking Press, 1941.

———. *The Oppermanns.* Trans. James Cleugh. New York: Carroll & Graf, 1983.

Fittko, Lisa. *Escape Through the Pyrenees.* Trans. David Koblick. Evanston, Ill.: Northwestern University Press, 2000.

Frank, Anne. *The Diary of a Young Girl.* Trans. Susan Massotty. Ed. Otto H. Frank and Mirjam Pressler. New York: Bantam Books, 1991.

Fry, Varian. *Assignment: Rescue, An Autobiography.* New York: Scholastic in conjunction with the United States Holocaust Memorial Museum, 1968.

———. *Surrender on Demand.* Boulder, Colo.: Johnson Books in conjunction with the United States Holocaust Memorial Museum, 1997.

———. *The Peace That Failed: How Europe Sowed the Seeds of War.* New York: Foreign Policy Association, 1939.

Gold, Mary Jayne. *Crossroads Marseilles 1940.* Garden City, N.Y.: Doubleday, 1980.

Green, Joshua M., and Shiva Kumar in consultation with Joanne Weiner

Rudof, ed. *Witness: Voices from the Holocaust*. New York. Simon & Schuster in association with the Fortunoff Video Archive for Holocaust Testimonies, Yale University, 2000.

Greenberg, Karen J., ed. Columbia University Library, Varian Fry Papers. *Archives of the Holocaust: An International Collection of Selected Documents*, vol. 5. New York: Garland Publishing, 1990.

Guggenheim, Peggy. *Out of This Century: Confessions of an Art Addict*. 2nd ed. Paperback: Andre Deutsch, 1985. Printed in the United States.

Heiden, Konrad. *Der Fuehrer*. Trans. Ralph Manheim. Boston: Houghton Mifflin, 1994.

Hirschman, Albert O. *A Propensity to Self-Subversion*. Cambridge, Mass.: Harvard University Press, 1995.

Hitler, Adolf. *Mein Kampf*. Trans. Ralph Manheim. New York: Houghton Mifflin, 1971. First Mariner Books, 1999.

Isenberg, Sheila. *A Hero of our Own: The Story of Varian Fry*. New York: Random House, 2001.

Kirstein, Lincoln. *Mosaic: Memoirs*. New York: Farrar, Straus and Giroux, 1994.

Klein, Gerda Weissmann. *All But My Life*. New York: Hill and Wang, 1957.

Langer, Lawrence L. *Holocaust Testimonies: the Ruins of Memory*. New Haven: Yale University Press, 1991.

Marino, Andy. *A Quiet American: The Secret War of Varian Fry*. New York: St. Martin's Press, 1999.

McCabe, Cynthia Jaffee. "Wanted by the Gestapo: Saved by America—Varian Fry and the Emergency Rescue Committee." *The Muses Flee Hitler: Cultural Transfer and Adaptation 1930–1945*. Ed. Jarrell C. Jackman and Carla M. Borden. Washington, D.C.: Smithsonian Institution Press, 1983.

Mehring, Walter. *No Road Back*. Trans. S. A. DeWitt. New York: Samuel Curl, 1944.

Mehring, Walter. *The Lost Library: The Autobiography of a Culture*. Trans. Richard and Clara Winston. New York: Bobbs-Merrill, 1951.

Meyerhof, Walter. *In the Shadow of Love: Stories from My Life*. Santa Barbara, Calif.: Fithian Press, 2002.

Paldiel, Mordecai. "Varian Fry, the American Who Saved Thousands in France." *Saving the Jews: Amazing Stories of Men and Women Who Defied the "Final Solution."* Rockville, Md.: Schreiber Publishing, 2000.

Pauli, Hertha. *Break of Time.* New York: Hawthorn Books, 1972.

Pisar, Samuel. *Of Blood and Hope.* Boston: Little, Brown, 1980.

Ryan, Donna. *The Holocaust & The Jews of Marseille: The Enforcement of Anti-Semitic Policies in Vichy France.* Chicago: University of Illinois Press, 1996.

Sahl, Hans. *The Few and the Many.* Trans. Richard and Clara Winston. New York: Harcourt, Brace and World, 1962.

Serge, Victor. *Memoirs of a Revolutionary.* Trans. Peter Sedgwick. New York: Writers and Readers Publishing, 1984.

Schroeder, Peter W., and Dagmar Schroeder-Hildebrand. *Six Million Paper Clips: The Making of a Children's Holocaust Memorial.* Minneapolis: Kar-Ben Publishing, 2004.

Werfel, Alma Mahler. *And the Bridge Is Love.* New York: Harcourt, Brace, 1958.

Wiesel, Elie. *Night.* Trans. Marion Wiesel. New ed. New York: Hill and Wang, 2006. (1st pub. New York: Hill and Wang, 1958.)

Wyman, David S. *Paper Walls: America and the Refugee Crisis 1938–1941.* New York: Pantheon Books, 1985.

[Newspapers and Magazines]

"Blames U.S. Delays for Refugee Perils." New York *Daily News*, November 3, 1941.

Deal, Renee. "Shining a Light on an Unsung Hero." *Menlo Park's Almanac.* vol. 75, no. 40. October 1, 1997.

"Editor Describes Rioting in Berlin." *The New York Times*, July 17, 1935.

Frankel, Max. "Pimpernel, of the Press." *The New York Times Magazine*, November 23, 1997.

Fry, Varian. "Eyewitness Story of Berlin Horror." *New York Post*, July 16, 1935.

————. "The Massacre of Jews in Europe." *The New Republic*, December 1942, pp. 816–18.

"Property of Jews in Alsace Is Confiscated; Finer Furnishings Sent to Reich by Trainload." *The New York Times*, December 17, 1940.

"Record Marked Up at Seaplane Base." *The New York Times*, November 3, 1941.

Reston, James B. "Lisbon's Refugees Now Put at 8,000." *The New York Times*, December 15, 1940.

[Personal Communication]

Fry, Annette. E-mails to the author. 2006: August 24, 26; September 14, 24, 30; October 11, 19, 25; November 10, 23. 2007: January 12, 19.

Rosenberg, Dr. Justus (Gussie). E-mails to the author. 2007: May 4, 9, 20.

————. Telephone interview with the author. May 4, 2007.

Sauvage, Pierre. E-mails to the author. 2006: April 14, 16; May 3; July 10; August 16; September 17; October 16; November 14. 2007: March 19; April 3, 10, 25; June 17.

————. Personal interview with the author. August 2, 2006.

[Other]

Assignment: Rescue Study Guide. Varian Fry Foundation Project/IRC, An Educational Project of the International Rescue Committee. Walter Meyerhof, project manager. Menlo Park, Calif.: 1999.

Ebel, Miriam Davenport. *An Unsentimental Education: A Memoir*. Posted at www.varianfry.org with the permission of Dr. Charles Ebel. www.varian fry.org/ebel_en.htm. 1999.

Time magazine archives, July 3, 1933.

Varian Fry Papers, Rare Book and Manuscript Library, Columbia University.

[Video]

Assignment: Rescue—The Story of Varian Fry and the Emergency Rescue Committee. Narrated by Meryl Streep. Varian Fry Foundation Project/IRC and Richard Kaplan Productions. 1997.

And Crown Thy Good: Varian Fry in Marseille. Forthcoming documentary by Pierre Sauvage. A Varian Fry Institute / Chambon Foundation production.

Auschwitz Death Camp. Elie Wiesel with Oprah. Produced by Harpo, Inc., 2006.

Paper Clips. The Johnson Group, 2003.

The Exiles (1989). Documentary produced and directed by Richard Kaplan.

[Web Sites]

United States Holocaust Memorial Museum. www.ushmm.org

Varian Fry Institute. www.varianfry.org

Chambon Foundation. www.chambon.org

The History Place. World War Two in Europe, Timeline with photos and text. www.historyplace.com/worldwar2/timeline/ww2time.htm

RECOMMENDED FURTHER READING

Bartoletti, Susan Campbell. *Hitler Youth: Growing Up in Hitler's Shadow*. New York: Scholastic, 2005.
The story of young Germans trained to be Hitler Youth.

Fittko, Lisa. *Escape Through the Pyrenees*. Trans. David Koblick. Evanston, Ill.: Northwestern University Press, 2000.
The story of Lisa and Hans Fittko, including how they led refugees over the Pyrenees mountains who were sent to them by Varian Fry.

Frank, Anne. *The Diary of a Young Girl*. Trans. Susan Massotty. Ed. Otto H. Frank and Mirjam Pressler. New York: Bantam Books, 1991.
This diary of a Jewish teenager chronicles the time she spent in hiding with her family.

Fry, Varian. *Assignment: Rescue, An Autobiography*. New York: Scholastic in conjunction with the United States Holocaust Memorial Museum, 1968.
An abbreviated account of Varian Fry's work in Marseilles, written with a young reader in mind.

————. *Surrender on Demand*. Boulder, Colo.: Johnson Books in conjunction with the United States Holocaust Memorial Museum, 1997.
A memoir written by Varian Fry detailing his work in Marseilles.

Giblin, James Cross. *The Life and Death of Adolf Hitler*. New York: Clarion Books, 2002.

Lobel, Anita. *No Pretty Pictures*. New York: Greenwillow Books, 1998.
A memoir by a child Holocaust survivor.

Wiesel, Elie. *Night*. Trans. Marion Wiesel. New ed. New York: Hill and Wang, 2006.
Nobel Prize–winning author Elie Wiesel describes his experiences in a Nazi concentration camp.

RECOMMENDED WEB SITES

The Web site for the United States Holocaust Memorial Museum, located in Washington, D.C., contains a wealth of information about the Holocaust, including photographs, testimonies, videos, maps, teaching resources, and much more.
www.ushmm.org

Yad Vashem, located in Jerusalem, Israel, documents the history of the Jewish people during the Holocaust and preserves the memory of each one of the six million Jews who were murdered.
www.yadvashem.org

The History Place has a chronological timeline of World War II, including photographs.
www.historyplace.com/worldwar2/timeline/ww2time.htm

The Varian Fry Institute has information about Varian Fry and his co-workers in Marseilles and links to related material.
www.varianfry.org

Learn more about Le Chambon, the French mountain village where five thousand Jews were sheltered and protected by five thousand Christians.
www.chambon.org

A Teacher's Guide to the Holocaust, produced by the Florida Center for Instructional Technology, is a great Web site for anyone interested in learning more about the Holocaust. It has virtual-reality movies that allow you to view 360 degrees inside concentration camps such as Auschwitz, Birkenau, and Dachau; a timeline with pop-up definitions and verbal pronunciations of both English and German words; photographs, video clips, music files, historical documents, and Web links. It also has teacher resources such as lesson plans and student activities.
http://fcit.coedu.usf.edu/holocaust

The International Rescue Committee, successor to the organization that sent Varian Fry to Marseilles, continues to help refugees from all over the world.
www.theirc.org

Find out why students in Whitwell, Tennessee, decided to collect one paper clip for each Jew killed during the Holocaust and build a memorial in an authentic German railroad car. Learn more about The Children's Holocaust Memorial and Paper Clip Project at Whitwell Middle School.
http://69.8.250.59/homepage_pc.cfm?id=78

ACKNOWLEDGMENTS

I would like to thank the following people for assisting me with photographs, information, and research material; this book would not have been possible without their help: Annette Riley Fry, who kindly shared family photographs with me and allowed me to use Varian Fry's personal correspondence; Pierre Sauvage, President of the Varian Fry Institute and Chambon Foundation; Dr. Justus Rosenberg, who graciously described to me his days with Varian Fry; Mira Perrizo, Publisher of Johnson Books; Marilyn Small, Rights and Permissions Department, Scholastic Inc.; Maren Read and Caroline Waddell, Photo Reference Coordinators at the United States Holocaust Memorial Museum; Michael Ryan, Tara Craig, and Jennifer Lee at the Rare Book and Manuscript Library at Columbia University; Rutha Beamon at the National Archives and Records Administration Still Picture Reference Department; Katherine Sarkis and Ronnie Saha at the International Rescue Committee; Fran O'Donnell, Curator of Archives and Manuscripts, Andover-Harvard Theological Library, Harvard Divinity School; Michaela Ullmann, Feuchtwanger Curator, University of Southern California; Jennifer Belt, Art Resource; Susan Shirley at the William F. Laman Library in North Little Rock, Arkansas; and Brittney McClafferty, my research assistant while visiting Columbia University. I'd also like to thank my editor, Beverly Reingold, and my copy editor, Elaine Chubb, for their discerning guidance.

ILLUSTRATION CREDITS

The photographs on pages 21, 40, 49, 71, 96, 104, 105, 109, 111, 114, 125, 131, 132, 147, 149, and 161 were provided by the Varian Fry Institute, which also provided the image that appears as the frontispiece and again on page 66, a photograph of Varian Fry taken by Ylla (Camilla Koffler: 1911–1955), copyright © Pryor Dodge.

The photographs on pages 9 (courtesy of B. Ashley Grimes II), 10 (courtesy of Estelle Bechoefer), 47 (Albert Hirschman, source), 62 (Daniel Bénédite, source), 68 (courtesy of Donald Carroll), 87 (Miriam Davenport Ebel, source), 103 (Daniel Bénédite, source), 134 (courtesy of Cynthia Jaffee McCabe), and 157 (courtesy of Yad Vashem) were provided by the United States Holocaust Memorial Museum, which also provided the image of the Nazi parade that appears on the jacket and again on page 5, a photograph taken by Varian Fry in 1935, from the personal collection of Annette Fry.

The photograph of Varian Fry on the jacket and on page 3, as well as the photographs on pages 22, 160, and 164, appear courtesy of Annette Fry, and are from her personal collection.

The photographs on pages 8 (both: photo no. 306-NT-177-708c, photo no. 242-HB-1340), 11 (photo no. 242-HLB-5073-20), and 158 (photo no. 238-NT-592) were provided by the National Archives.

The image of the lithograph by Jacques Lipchitz on page 163 appears courtesy of the International Rescue Committee, *Flight* portfolio.

The photograph on page 38 appears courtesy of the Feuchtwanger Memorial Library, Special Collections, University of Southern California Libraries.

The image on page 110 is a photograph taken by Ylla (Camilla Koffler: 1911–1955), from the Museum of Modern Art Archives, New York: gift of

Mrs. Varian Fry; courtesy of the Museum of Modern Art and Pryor Dodge; copyright © Pryor Dodge.

The photograph of Gussie on page 50 appears courtesy of Professor Justus Rosenberg.

INDEX